From One Winning Career to the Next

From One Winning Career to the Next

Transitioning Public Sector Leadership and Security Expertise to the Business Bottom Line

J. David Quilter

ELSEVIER

AMSTERDAM • BOSTON • HEIDELBERG • LONDON
NEW YORK • OXFORD • PARIS • SAN DIEGO
SAN FRANCISCO • SINGAPORE • SYDNEY • TOKYO

Security
Executive Council

Elsevier

The Boulevard, Langford Lane, Kidlington, Oxford, OX5 1GB, UK

225 Wyman Street, Waltham, MA 02451, USA

Originally published by the Security Executive Council, 2008

Copyright © 2013 The Security Executive Council. Published by Elsevier Inc.

Notices

Knowledge and best practice in this field are constantly changing. As new research and experience broaden our understanding, changes in research methods, professional practices, or medical treatment may become necessary.

Practitioners and researchers must always rely on their own experience and knowledge in evaluating and using any information, methods, compounds, or experiments described herein. In using such information or methods they should be mindful of their own safety and the safety of others, including parties for whom they have a professional responsibility.

To the fullest extent of the law, neither the Publisher nor the authors, contributors, or editors, assume any liability for any injury and/or damage to persons or property as a matter of products liability, negligence or otherwise, or from any use or operation of any methods, products, instructions, or ideas contained in the material herein.

British Library Cataloguing in Publication Data

A catalogue record for this book is available from the British Library

Library of Congress Cataloging-in-Publication Data

A catalog record for this book is available from the Library of Congress

ISBN: 978-0-12-411594-1

For more publications in the Elsevier Risk Management and Security Collection, visit our website at **store.elsevier.com/SecurityExecutiveCouncil**

This book has been manufactured using Print On Demand technology. Each copy is produced to order and is limited to black ink. The online version of this book will show color figures where appropriate.

CONTENTS

ACKNOWLEDGMENTS

Life for me has always been based on relationships; first with family, then with friends and colleagues. What is between these pages is in many ways a result of the good fortune and richness of my life. My values and work ethic I learned from Tom Quilter—my dad. My mom, Rose Quilter, gave me encouragement and a wealth of empathetic understanding. As a middle child, I spent a lot of time getting into (and out of) trouble, which gave me a good sense of how to make my own way.

My life has been shaped by the love and support of three sisters and two brothers. Over the years, we have become closer and at the same time we honor the uniqueness of the different paths each has chosen. I owe a special debt to RoseMarie Quilter, RSCJ, who joined me in the work of this book. I am blessed with three wonderful sons who have further enriched my life, brought me great joy, and added to my being much more tenacious. My strong and determined partner Elizabeth is my best friend.

There are many teams and individuals who have been special in my work life, and some who have become true friends. I will thank you individually, but want to acknowledge the privilege of working with and for colleagues like Ray Halperin, who early in my career insisted that I had to learn to write better, and Jack Lawn, who backed me up many times during my DEA career. When I stepped out into corporate America it was leaders like Bob DeBaun and Peter Fazio who helped me understand the nuances in corporate cultures. Executive leadership from Joe Damico and Lester Knight gave me a model of how to be both genuine and effective in business practice. We surround ourselves with stronger, brighter people when we want to succeed and my teams have proven this fact time after time. Paul Herring and Jim Miller are two of the strongest and brightest around.

I am most fortunate to be associated with the smart, caring, and creative people who comprise the Security Executive Council and am particularly indebted to Bob Hayes and Kathleen Kotwica for helping make this book-dream a reality.

Gratefully,
J. David Quilter
Baldwinsville, NY

Prologue

What's past is prologue.

William Shakespeare

The world of business powerfully influenced my early life. As a middle child, the third of six, I was often on my own and teachers described me as a daydreamer. I recall at the age of four dreaming of owning my own business. I had an imaginary employee, Harry, who worked at "mine ossuf." This office was located in any parking lot that had a hut.

My dad was a big influence on me. His career was in the wholesale distribution business. He sold two of the great brands available after World War II—RCA Victor and Whirlpool—as well as many small appliances. For 53 years, dad worked in the home entertainment and appliance business. He sold products that spanned everything from 1930 Victrolas and manual washing machines to the first color TVs and VCRs.

Dad's business friends were frequent guests at our dinner table. They ranged from executives of large companies to sales employees and loading dock workers. We were coached on good manners and taught to listen to adult conversations. These included every possible aspect of how businesses were built: profit and loss, advertising strategies, sales training, dealing with unions, employee hiring and firing, etc. The things my father had to think about seemed endless. I found all this fascinating and loved to go with him to "the place," which was the way our family referred to his office.

From the late 1940s, we lived in Syracuse, New York: the hub of the Empire State. In those years, Syracuse was like a small Chicago; there were flourishing manufacturing and service industries, good schools, including Syracuse University and Le Moyne College, excellent sports teams, and a pervasive sense of community. I loved growing up in central New York and I still enjoy large snow drifts.

A thoroughly competitive retail environment, our city was often chosen as a test market by companies launching new products. General Electric had thousands of employees at its Electronics Park manufacturing plants, where most GE televisions were made, and every employee could get discounts on products. Because competition was intense, Syracuse was a tough business environment for appliance sales.

I became more aware of the challenges dad faced when, in 1958, I went with him on a buying trip for the new RCA line. He bought several million dollars worth of radios, high fidelity record players, black and white TVs as well as RCA's newest color TVs, and stereo systems. After a full day of purchasing meetings we went back to the hotel. As we were going up to our room I said in awe, "Dad, you just bought millions of dollars of product." Delighted, he laughed, and said, "Oh, that's the easy part—now I have to sell everything I just bought and make a profit. That's what business is all about: making a profit."

As I reflect back on those times some indelible impressions remain. My father toiled 5 days a week and a half-day every Saturday. At the age of 17 he began as a clerk, then moved into sales, and finally into executive management. He stayed with his company for 53 years. More importantly, he knew the business from the bottom up. He mastered and monitored its every aspect, from accounts to parts inventory. He mentored every employee, especially those involved in sales and customer service. He was directly involved in employee relations and labor negotiations. He learned the business from the ground up and then taught it to those around him, including his kids. Even at the dinner table.

Several times throughout my federal career I thought of leaving government service to jump into the business world. In fact, some of my closest friends in Drug Enforcement Administration (DEA) said, "DQ, what the heck are you doing working for the government, you could be making real money in business." My answer was always the same: "The government and our citizens need good people who care about what they do, folks with solid values, who work hard and believe in and respect what we are doing." I completed a wonderful 26-year career in the service of my country in late 1993. I had served 3 years as a Marine Corps officer with a tour in Vietnam, and for the next 23 years I was a Special Agent and Supervisory Special Agent in the DEA.

During this time, the business lessons my father instilled in me had not been lost. When I finally decided to move from my government career into the business world, I was committed to using the lessons I had learned from my dad and throughout my life, to using my knowledge, skills, and abilities to make a *profit* for whatever organization that hired me.

I was fortunate to move into security leadership. True business acumen has everything to do with being a successful security leader in today's down-sized, right-sized, and outsourced business operations. It's about knowing how to help the organization be more profitable. It's about assisting operational leaders to be more successful by addressing issues such as disgruntled or threatening customers or employees. It's about dealing with a wide variety of theft, embezzlement, and violence issues.

It is only through learning and knowing the business that one can tailor security measures to the realities of the corporate environment. That is where effectiveness lies. Smart security solutions mitigate business risks and improve business profitability.

I have sometimes been asked how I became successful developing security programs that focus so well on the needs of different businesses. The answer is simple. By the time I was 16, I had earned the equivalent of an MBA from one of my toughest and best teachers, my father. Everything I have done in corporate security has been focused on being a business partner. I have lived by my father's mantra: "Show up every day, learn the business, be honest, and work like hell!"

I wrote this book to help you transition from a government and/or military service career to corporate culture, so that you too can be successful as a business-focused security leader. There are also additional applications for the information on these pages. If you are hiring a security leader for a business, this book will help you target the right person. In the post-9/11 world, if you are responsible for any major institution, such as a school or hospital, this book will be useful in many ways. Perhaps, you are simply a lifelong learner. I welcome you to this journey.

This book is for those who:

• are transitioning from a government or military position to business security leadership,

- want to understand why security leadership is a priority in the post-9/11 world,
- are the administrator or executive of any educational, financial, industrial, or healthcare institution,
- want to understand the new paradigm of security leadership, and especially how a true security leader can positively impact the corporation's "bottom line,"
- are concerned about the safety and well-being of your employees and clients,
- need to hire a skilled security professional to analyze, foresee, mitigate, and prevent crises in their organizations,
- or are lifelong learners and enjoy thinking outside the box.

A Security Leader's Journey

It can be confusing and challenging for security leaders to step into organizational environments that they do not adequately understand. They may fail to adjust their talents and the resulting frustration for them and the business often have a negative impact on both. This is especially true for individuals in transition from government or military careers who step into a corporate or nongovernment organization (NGO).

Before you accept this challenge, it is imperative for you to assess your background, knowledge, and skills in view of the great new opportunity facing you, that is, if you are going to make a positive impact. In this chapter, I'll share my journey as a security leader. My intent is to help you move forward with your eyes and ears well tuned to the challenges that lie ahead.

When I completed my Drug Enforcement Administration (DEA) service, I was very, very hungry. I knew I had the right stuff to be the head of corporate security for a very large organization. But how could I find that right opportunity? How could I break into corporate America, have an impact, and continue to grow personally and professionally?

This is my journey from committed and effective government servant to someone who over the course of a dozen years built security programs that have been described as outstanding and that have established business-smart security initiatives and created a new security environment for employees and operations.

Over the years these programs have recovered millions of lost dollars, reinforced sound ethical values, established high standards that support one and all—from contract employees to executives. My one goal was to create a security environment that would increase profits while protecting everyone in the company. This is no easy task.

1.1 COMPANY ONE

So let's start at the beginning. When I was close to government retirement, I was recruited by the owners of a small privately-held service company that I'll call Company One. The business employed 35 people and conducted operations in three states. I had come to know the owners through a series of money laundering prevention presentations that they attended. They felt that I had the team-building skills they needed and assured me I could lead their business as chief executive officer (CEO) and president. They seemed committed to a disciplined transformation of their organization. Several knowledgeable friends looked at the firm's business fundamentals and financials with a critical eye, and each of them urged me to accept the opportunity. The owners attended my DEA retirement dinner and publicly announced they were thrilled to have me join their company and help reshape it. What an ideal opportunity and what a wake-up call!

My jump into a small privately-held company was immediate. I went from DEA on Friday to my new office on Monday. There was a lot of work to do, and I got right to it. I had A.J. Seelhammer, a close friend with years of financial, marketing, sales, and strategic planning experience, to facilitate the company's first business strategy session. We needed to determine how to change the whole series of internal, financial, and operational processes that kept this company continually on the brink of financial failure.

I soon discovered that a number of employees did not know the capabilities of some of the systems they were using, and most had only a basic understanding of how to operate them. It turned out that someone told them there was no time to be trained. They had to get the work done according to their personal whims. Basic processes were haphazard: who did what, how follow-up with customers happened, or when products were shipped was anyone's guess. Customers were angry. What a way to treat the people who paid the bills!

After a few months and many team meetings—a new concept—we were ready to take on some major issues like cash flow. We reduced the daily averages of payments on accounts receivable from 120 days to less than 25 days. At one point, we even had the receivables averaging less than 10 days. All it took was effective communication and recognizing the skills and contributions of the employees. They loved it and so did I. Even after this significant progress, within a few months I identified that the major problem with this business was the owners.

One of the guiding principles in a small business is "cash is king." But these owners had a different perspective. They treated the corporate check book as their private check book. Whenever they had an idea they went out and spent money because, in their words, "just one good idea can make a lot of money." They were not short of ideas but they were short on cash. What they called intuitive investment I called reckless spending. Their lack of fiscal discipline resulted in my putting them on notice. They would have to get my written approval prior to funds being obligated.

That did not sit well because they owned the company. On top of that, I discovered the vice president of finance had decided, independently, to skip some quarterly internal revenue service (IRS) payroll tax payments. This had been hidden from me for several months. When I confronted the vice president I said: "The next time you hide something from me you're fired." That didn't go over well either. The employee had been with the company for many years and of course informed the owners. They thought I was overreacting.

I didn't care much about what the owners thought. I was literally not sleeping nights and sweating out every payday because cash flow was so tight. Every day for several months when the mail arrived I had it delivered to my desk so that I would know what was going on. Invariably there were more accounts payables than receivables.

While this was one heck of a jump into the world of business, the lessons learned, the analysis done, and saying to employees "I don't know if we will have a pay check for you this month" all gave me a unique perspective on what it takes to make a business succeed. I was routinely in the office before 6:00 a.m. to study how customer service and back-office operations worked. Teamwork with employees was being established on clear terms. Customers were considerably happier.

However, my relationship with the owners got worse every week. Their ideas never stopped and I never gave in. After 11 months the relationship was over. I was fired on Halloween. For the first time in 25 years, I was out of work.

From this memorable experience I learned that career changes are not for the faint of heart. The first transition can be difficult, even if you have carefully assessed the opportunity.

One of the keys to being a strong security leader is to have a fundamental ethics and values match between you, the executive and senior leaders, and the organization as a whole. When the chips are down and issues start spinning out of control, you will find out who in the organization really trusts you. I found this out the hard way in Company One.

Fortunately, even in the midst of disappointment, I was grounded from previous life-shaping experiences: my family, the Marine Corps, and DEA had prepared me well for life's challenges. From this first less-than-glorious introduction to the business world, my formative experiences gave me the balance, stability, and strength to sustain me through major struggles.

After my trick-or-treat experience with Company One, I took a considerable period of time to reflect on my personal and professional priorities. This was not easy, but I felt I needed to mine the situation for insight. I found myself thinking about my years in Vietnam. My gut told me that I needed to apply some of the practical lessons learned in the extreme circumstances of war to the realities of making a business work and to integrating security goals within that business.

I remembered that as a young First Lieutenant in the Marines I was selected to head a Civic Action Team (CA-Team) outside the wire near our Da Nang Air Base in Vietnam. The biggest part of the job was to rebuild a sense of community, keep the peace, and keep both Viet Cong and North Vietnamese Army activity out of our tactical area and away from the air base. The really effective decisions in Da Nang could not have been learned from any pacification manual or by attending some United States Agency for International Development (USAID) school. Good choices came from meeting with the village elders and hamlet council, seeing what made sense to them, and supporting them in attaining their goals. The first thing they wanted was medical help for the children and the elders, especially for skin diseases, which were rampant.

Our CA-Team recruited one of the few dermatologists in the region. We had to convince the doctor, an Army Major with 95th Med Evac Unit, along with his medical team to provide weekly medical civic action program (MEDCAPs) to the villagers in Hoa, a hamlet that was a part of Phuoc Tuong Village; this area was also called Dog Patch by most Marines, a few miles away. With the MEDCAPs up and running, the villagers knew we had listened to them and delivered. In a few weeks, we were treating several hundred villagers during our 4-hour Wednesday MEDCAPs.

That was an early opportunity to figure out what needed to happen and to deliver the right result. It came from listening to the real needs and then getting results. This team effort improved our effectiveness and subsequently kept us safe. In this instance, and those subsequently, the dynamics of both opportunity and understanding the culture helped me to figure out what needed to be done, and I did it. Most of the challenging situations I have faced since Vietnam have been constant in one respect: there is very little routine guidance, no clear path.

In Company One, the owners did not know how to effectively address, or they wanted to avoid, the integrity issues facing the organization. Such problems were messy. In later settings, I sometimes saw similar patterns of avoidance. Even though corporate leaders realized that complex security issues had to be dealt with in a fair and respectful way, such security scenarios had never been a part of any MBA program; they were not seen as career enhancers.

So part of my learning from the Company One experience was to work with people who would trust me to get the job done. In order to do the job, I had to listen to everybody involved in the organization to accomplish meaningful results. Such results require teamwork at every level of the organization. I also learned that once a management team trusted me, they would increasingly rely on me to manage challenging business issues, even those that are indirectly related to security. Little did I know that the time I took to rethink my priorities early in my business career would become a basic building block for future success in corporate America. What appeared to be a disappointing trick became a treat, another opportunity as I continued my journey of learning.

1.2 COMPANY TWO

In retrospect, I see that I had compressed wonderful business and life lessons in those 10 months. However, at the time, it seemed that the wheels had fallen off my bike. The depression and discouragement I felt and the near free-fall of this experience led to a new resolve. I relied on my family, my close friends, and many professional colleagues for support and advice. Little by little, I began to see the forest, not just the trees. I learned I would only achieve success by working with people who held values compatible with mine. I knew how to work. I had many skills that I would be able to contribute to the business world but on my own terms.

I had a deep inner sense that I needed to keep doing the right things day in and day out. I was tenacious. As difficult as this period was, I had confidence that life was about to change. And it did. After a considerable period reflecting on my next job, I began doing research. At first, I looked at opportunities all over the country. Finally, I realized I must narrow my job search. So I defined it as follows:

- Move from Texas to Chicago.
- Look at firms with major operations within 20 miles of my Chicago zip code.
- Select firms with at least 10,000 employees.
- Seek companies with annual revenue of at least $500,000,000.

One day I plugged these parameters into the computer and it came up with the names, addresses, and phone numbers of 2,400 companies. I realized that the right opportunity awaited me in Chicago; all I had to do was find it.

Within a few months, I had relocated from the Southwest and immediately developed a business plan. In retrospect, this was critical. This was my goal: in 36 months or less, I would be a recognized security leader in Chicago or the Midwest.

At Company Two, the approach to security was essentially to wait for the phone to ring. The executives were reactive to events that had already taken a toll on the business. Because my position was outsourced, there was virtually no money to travel and learn about the business. I discovered that the position had been designed to fulfill some of the requirements of insurance policies. They wanted someone to look into things after they happened. I used to joke that when I got the call, not only was the horse out of the barn but also the barn had burned down, and if there was anything to follow up on, the evidence had been contaminated, lost, or thrown out.

In this firm, every aspect of the business was focused on making the financial numbers work. The leadership of the company was split between folks focused purely on financials and leaders who sought to care for the needs of customers and employees. Both groups were committed to making the business succeed. The latter group believed we must give more than we get and leave more than we take.

As the director of security, I had been with the company only a few months when I was asked to meet a senior executive who was selected to become the chairman of a new spin-off company ("New Co"). The purpose of our meeting was to discuss security strategies and how the soon-to-be-spun-off company's operations could effectively address security issues.

By this time I had a sense that the priorities of Company Two were not going to be a good fit for my values. When I met with the soon-to-be new chairman, I laid out a very simple but direct plan on how a smart approach to security could contribute to the overall success of New Co. I described key challenges for elements of New Co's business that remained intertwined with the parent company. We discussed several different challenges for New Co as this global business made its debut in the market place. Although I did not know it at the time, the chairman was interviewing me to be the security leader for New Co. After less than an hour, I was asked to join this five billion dollar spin-off. Over the next year, I served both Company Two as an outsourced director of security and New Co, which became Company Three, as its director of security. This continued until we recruited someone to step in as my replacement with Company Two.

During my first months with these companies, every day was an adventure. I never forgot my dad's mantra: show up every day, learn the business, be honest, and work like hell. While I knew that learning the business was paramount, the phone began ringing regularly about security issues. Word had gotten out that I could help. Sometimes you get lucky. I was soon presented with a large embezzlement case. This was a wonderful opportunity to convince the business folks that security could impact the bottom line.

1.3 COMPANY THREE

Because I was conscious of being new to the organization, initially I tended to hang back and observe. It was almost as though I instinctively preferred surveillance to engaging with others immediately. The CEO quickly changed that. From the time I was brought on board, I was attending key portions of executive meetings, and he personally introduced me to all the executives. Subsequently, if there was an open seat on the corporate jet, I was invited on trips as he knew the importance of a sound business orientation.

I carefully observed how the new executives of Company Three interacted on business issues during the period as it was spun-off. I began to appreciate their good sense and dedication. I also noted little self-seeking ego in their exchanges with one another and with me: they were approachable and focused on growing the business.

This was so even though the security function was new and most of the business leaders did not know how security could contribute to the success of their operations or what it could do for them. Executives, managers, supervisors, and employees asked tough questions and when given a reasonable response, they appreciated what was said and its value. They wanted me to succeed personally as well as professionally.

Remember this: success relates to the culture of the company. By this point for me the culture mattered more than salary, title, benefits, or location. The culture of the place can make or break your efforts.

As a member of an outstanding human resources (HR) team, a good place for a security leader to locate, I had unlimited access to the people issues across the entire enterprise. Because I had adequate information, as well as the trust of my peers, we soon recovered over $200,000 in funds that had been embezzled by a trusted long-term employee.

Actually, prior to this early win, the new chief operating officer (COO) and president of Company Three had not been enthusiastic to have a full-time security leader on his team. He was not in opposition to the goals of security; he was simply pragmatic. He saw security purely as expense and overhead. His role among the executives was to ensure that every aspect of the business contributed to the bottom line and applied the disciplinary glue. Company Three's senior leaders had to convince him that their business plans were enhancing profits. As I quickly found out, this included security initiatives.

The COO was polished and likeable. He was a highly respected leader with over 20 years of experience in every aspect of the business and he never minced words. Although some may have found this trait intimidating, I approached every meeting with the COO as an opportunity to learn. I liked his directness. I knew he was sharing things as he saw them. I learned a great deal from him and from others like him. It was refreshing to be with someone who never beat around the bush. He was tough, but always professional. I sensed that he would tell me what he expected; he would also give me a chance to meet those expectations. He was amazed at the recovery of embezzled funds because of our security work.

Once you deliver results and gain the respect of senior leaders, they become your greatest allies. I was fortunate that they saw how we handled the sensitive matter of the embezzlement (this will be further discussed in Chapter 2). They threw their full support behind the security program. The chairman made it crystal clear to every leader that when they identified any business issue where security was a factor, I was to be briefed immediately. What he said was carried out to the letter. The culture of the organization gave responsibility and accountability to every employee. While each ran a segment of the business in a disciplined and creative way, cooperation was also normative. I never sensed an "us against them" or management against employee tension. By this point the umbilical cord to Company Two had been cut and we were on our own to sink or succeed.

When the Company Three spin-off was complete, I became the full-time security director. Company Three from day one was a multibillion-dollar manufacturing and distribution business. Eventually, we had a three-person security team that functioned like a well-oiled clock. Each of us had different skills and each was able to lead in various ways. We were focused on designing our security program to complement and support the company's global business goals and operations.

It didn't start out like that. When I joined Company Three, they had no, and I mean no, coordinated security function. They had many alarms, access control systems, and guards. But all security functions and services had been outsourced for years to a highly regarded national facilities management firm. In 1996, that was not unusual. In fact, it was part of an entrenched business mentality about security operations, namely, that security is an expense so minimize it. Expectations for the security function had traditionally been low, and did not include any proactive or pro-business role.

Prior to 9/11, company leaders who understood that security could add to the bottom line, rather than detract from it, usually arrived at this conclusion through a catastrophic event. Some calamity hit them in the face. It was traumatic. If the organization survived, and many did not, management knew it had dodged a bullet. Often, even in a less traumatic scenario, there was a tremendous loss of reputation, time, and money. This was normative until September 11, 2001. In the aftermath of WorldCom, Enron, and 9/11, regulatory entities passed an avalanche of industry-impacting legislations. Employees and shareholders asked embarrassing questions. CEOs began to reevaluate the need for proactive security integrated across their businesses.

Even today in some corporate circles, be prepared to be met with wariness, not because people don't like you but because they don't know you. Their concept of security may still be that you are the corporate cop. Most people feel uncomfortable around cops. This is exacerbated if you are new to the organization and the security function itself is new. Be ready for considerable internal marketing and sales. This is your chance to begin to show creativity. If you do it right, it will be fulfilling, it will prepare others to trust you and, trust me, it will be fun.

There is nothing more important for the senior security leader than having a close professional relationship with those in charge of the organization. Because I enjoyed this relationship with executives at Company Three, my corporate experience there was effective for the company and life changing for me. The lead security position is rarely at C-level. It may be at the executive level or senior management level but the important consideration is that the security leader has close rapport and easy access to the chairman, CEO, general counsel, and others. In emergencies, decisions must be made in consultation *and* the security leader should have a leading and somewhat independent voice in calling the shots. Such flexibility depends on trust earned in advance.

A few months after I joined Company Three I was asked to host a meeting of Asset Protection Executives (APEX), a regional security organization of which I was a new member. APEX members are a select group of senior security leaders and multibillion dollar corporations, primarily in the greater Chicago area.

I arranged to have our meeting at Company Three's new conference center located on the executive floor of our headquarters. On the morning of the meeting, I informed the president's executive assistant of the meeting, gave her the agenda and list of the attendees. I suggested that if the president had a few minutes, and wished to stop by to make some remarks, he would be most welcome. I was not surprised when he entered the room as I was reviewing the day's agenda with participants.

I thought he might wish to share our business goals and speak of the recent spin-off challenges from Company Two. After saying that he appreciated the opportunity of addressing APEX, he mentioned how much he had learned about security and asset protection over the preceding few months. He shared his initial misgivings about employing a security team and detailed his former opinion that security was merely a drain on profits. Then, to my surprise, he said: "That's until Dave came to work on our executive team."

He attributed his previous expectations to not having had the benefit of a coworker who could help him and other business leaders appreciate the impact of a business-smart security program. He said he looked forward to working with our security team to deliver better business results. Then he thanked all the security executives in the room for what they were doing to help their organizations to reach their business goals, and he thanked me and the group for the opportunity to address our meeting.

The immediate reaction of several in the room was "how the heck did you get him to say that?" Many shared that after several years at their organizations, they had never had any executive appreciate their work so accurately, or realize that a security program, with the right drivers and the right executive leadership, could not only produce solid security results but also deliver excellent business outcomes.

When you join a company, it is important to seek out two or three security issues that are potential quick wins for the business. Discovering these issues may be challenging. In order to discover how to begin, keep the goals of the business in mind, become the person who wants to help others solve problems such as theft, threats, and shrinkage. Help them realize, through your actions, that you are there to help them keep the money they have worked hard to earn. For example, profits may leak out the backdoor and managers may be afraid to admit this. Such issues may have been in place longer than the managers. Prior to your arrival, employees may have had no one to help them take a serious look at how to address such losses. As a security leader, you can become their ally.

Sometimes, the simplest things can make a huge difference to security. For example, it matters that executives and senior leaders wear their company ID. A basic building block of effective physical access control is having employees wear one. When I joined Company Three they had 27,000 employees. At headquarters alone, over 4,000 persons were engaged in everything from manufacturing and sales to distribution and marketing. Management and many subcontractors also had access to our 230-acre campus. For many years there had been a policy that all employees, contractors, and visitors were to wear company IDs. Less than half complied with this policy.

I felt a change was in order if we were ever to manage physical access and begin to address other security issues. So our team went to the company's Internet site and downloaded the digital photos and unprotected signatures of our chairman and COO, and we created company IDs for them. Then they were invited to a private meeting to discuss company access control issues. Shortly afterward, I received a call saying they would come to my office the following morning.

When they arrived, they immediately saw their photos and signatures on ID cards placed on the conference table. We briefed them on a recent series of business and personal thefts by outsiders who had gained access to our facilities because we lacked a consistent security practice requiring everyone to wear IDs. A recent survey we conducted had confirmed that fewer than 50% of our employees were following company policy to display official IDs while on company property.

The COO then picked up his new ID card and asked how we were able to get his picture and signature. We explained how simple it was to download both. Access to signatures was restricted later that day.

Our team then requested the assistance of the chairman and the COO. We asked them to wear their company IDs. They looked at us for a very long time, stood up, and put on their IDs. They wore them regularly thereafter and personally asked other employees to do so. Their leadership in this simple matter marked a step in the right direction for security across the company, at no additional cost. They loved the no cost part.

I didn't know it at the time, but somehow I had landed on a corporate team that would prove to be exceptional. The executives I worked with at Company Three went on to be world-class leaders across their industry. The business challenges we faced for the next 3 years were massive. In that time, this team moved financial gains from marginal to spectacular. We worked like crazy, celebrated our milestones, delivered results based on values, and turned the business around. Can you tell why I loved working for Company Three?

The higher you go up in the organization, and especially with key members of the senior or executive management teams, the more focused and strategic the recommendations need to be. Again, the issue for the security leader is to know the business. A key mistake many new leaders make is to identify what they perceive as an issue in their area and then to quickly offer superficial solutions. You have to find smart business reasons for every aspect of security you intend to change. It is all about how you go about a change management model that first works for you, and in fact enhances security, or improves profits, or creates a new opportunity for the business. In business, it's not about security, it's about business. With smart, lean, security everyone wins.

This can be achieved by reconfiguring, cutting back, and in some cases modifying or even removing security that previously was in place—in some cases security that was costing millions of dollars year in, year out, for each operating cycle of the business. A sound security strategy, to be effective, has to be woven around and through the unique profit drivers of the business or organization if you are going to be successful. Every aspect of this is almost always a fight. This is a fight that must be won at several levels across the organization. Every security issue has to be resolved with long-term benefits and must be sustainable. There can be no slipups. In many cases, there are many operational leaders who are waiting for you to step on yourself and lose favor with those who brought you on board and thought you were the person for the job.

So how does one go about designing and then implementing changes to security in a large and often highly matrixed business or organization? What are the changes that enhance security and drive business success? One thing is for sure, change is slow. Whatever your original estimate is, double it. It takes patience, persistence, and a broad base of both business and security skills to really deliver a quality security program.

For the security leader, it will take leadership that is very flexible, values solid to the core, long days filled with a lot of hard work, and a willingness to take risks.

For me it took every skill I had ever learned, from the time I was a kid until now, coupled with an eagerness and willingness to learn more. Being a lifelong learner is absolutely essential for the security leader irrespective of his or her past credentials. Learning has to include equal doses of personal confidence and humility. By combining these two essential traits with sound security expertise, you have the ingredients that can transform the security in any business or organization. If it is pulled off successfully, you have the opportunity to move beyond security expertise to the realm of security know-how. It is know-how that catapults businesses' security initiatives from good to great. The same is true for the security leader with know-how. For me part of the fun is in the challenge: can I really improve the safety and security of the business and add to the bottom line?

1.4 COMPANY FOUR AND COMPANY FIVE

In today's corporate world, employees must adjust to change. After several months of hard work, Company Three had a security team of three working together with the seemingly effortless grace of seasoned athletes. When Company Three was acquired by Company Four, a number of security initiatives that our team had begun were adopted as "best security practices" by our new parent company. This gave our team and executives great satisfaction. As a team player and good corporate citizen, I knew I would play a key role in helping our team to integrate into Company Four's security effort. I also knew my role as the primary security leader was going to change.

I knew my role would be that of a senior security leader, but only as a member of a larger security team. This was a blow. I had worked hard to get where I was, and the business priorities and dynamics of the new parent company left me unsettled. I decided to wait until the right opportunity presented itself. I still wanted to be the alpha leader, the boss. A few months later, the call came. It was from a security recruiter who had contacted me many times over the years.

The recruiter said he had a client in the Chicago area eager to interview me. I met the general counsel of Company Five in Chicago. Company Five was a different and highly regulated industry, a multi-billion dollar corporation with operations in more than 15 states, as well as off-shore operations. I would be going from one industry to another; here was yet another opportunity to build a program from the ground up. After a 2-hour meeting, the move seemed right, but before I made a decision I wanted to meet with the chairman.

I had learned that to achieve results I needed open-door access all the way to the chairman's level. At this point in my career the only way I would consider a move would be if I had that kind of access. Otherwise, the cards would be stacked against me. Having learned this lesson very well throughout my government and corporate careers, I was not about to reverse the trend.

Within a week, I met with the general counsel and chairman of Company Five, who was also the CEO and president. Over lunch, I listened as they described their issues, and what they were looking for in a security leader. They wanted someone who could balance the needs of the business and security. Although Company Five was a seven billion dollar corporation with infrastructure stretching from the Southeast to the Northeast, they had no integrated security strategy. It looked like a great new opportunity.

If they wanted me, I had some requirements. First, I needed agreement on clear, reporting relationships acceptable to me. The chairman said that I would report to the general counsel. That was great, but I also expected to have a dotted line reporting relationship to the chairman and CEO. They assured me that I would have access to them whenever I wanted it. I would hold them to that several times over the next few years. Their question was—how long would it take me to build an effective security program across their organization? I estimated that it may take between 3 and 5 years. I admitted that it was a guess on my part because I didn't know the industry or business. I stated my goal was to learn their business, build a core security program, and be gone in 3–5 years. For me, time was of the essence.

At the end of this meeting, the chairman said "I'd like you to join our organization. Why don't you and the general counsel work out the details. We need someone with your proven know-how and security skills. I assure you, you will not only have my full support, but also the full support of our executive leadership team." I signed on with Company Five.

The meeting played out as I had hoped. I had done significant personal research on this company in preparation for this meeting. I knew I was well prepared. The opportunity gave me a chance to discover entirely new sets of problems and to bring effective solutions to the business table.

I also knew I was taking a risk. I did not have an adequate sense of the corporate culture I was stepping into. I was aware that their industry is a tough environment for nonoperational staff. However, I trusted the sincerity of both these two executive leaders; they were direct and honest. They had tried several times to recruit the right security leader to lead an internal start-up program. Difficult as this might be, I had the experience required. They assured me that they would help build their new security program.

In Company Five, I learned additional ways of aligning security with an organization's strategic values and goals. It also gave me opportunities to translate the business realities of their industry and design a security program that blended with operating plans of a different kind. I also learned the importance of understanding how much change a corporate culture can tolerate. If you are worth your salt, you will rock the boat.

Although executives may theoretically expect you to do this, they may not enjoy it in practice. Nevertheless, when you, as the security leader, demonstrate dollars saved, dollars recovered, or serious issues mitigated, you know the meaning of job satisfaction. Delivering these results puts security in the mainstream.

Corporate business environments vary from company to company and are a world apart from nonbusiness organizations. In corporate realignments, senior leaders disappear overnight. Usually, there is some form of corporate announcement that indicates they have "chosen to pursue other career opportunities."

This is significant because as you build your security program, especially from the ground up, you will have spent countless hours marketing your security vision and how it is going to improve the business operations these executives were leading. Then, in an instant, they are gone. Now you begin again with either one of their former direct reports, who has just been promoted, or someone who is new to the organization. The latter will have many of the same challenges you may have had when you joined the business.

If they are new to the organization I suggest you forget any serious meetings with them for about 3 months, because they are dealing with their own time constraints and need to establish themselves within the organization. Be realistic about the amount of time transitions required. If your background is in the government or the military, you are used to a voluntary/involuntary rotation of leaders, political appointments, or change of command ceremonies. Everyone in these and similar organizations knows its culture and has a basic trust in such customs. It is wise to be aware that business does not operate like this.

Be prepared to spend time with executives in two ways. First, use every opportunity wisely. At the same time do not waste their time. Before you meet with a senior leader, know what you want the outcome to be. They have hired you to help resolve business problems based on your management and security expertise. Secondly, place every conversation in a business context. Tie the issue you are dealing with to dollars saved, how to avoid risk, or how to best recover from the incident at hand. Present every concern in a concise format, without jargon, and with two or three options as possible resolutions to the problem. In subsequent meetings, demonstrate that your whole intent is to safeguard employees and improve morale while driving bottom line profitability. Frankness with a smile is essential.

During an early meeting with one CEO, I listened very carefully. Toward the end of our time I summed up my approach to security as follows: "I have earned all my grey hair. I want to work in an organization where I don't have to pull it out. My goals are to mitigate security exposures and risks; if I am selected to be the security leader I will need and expect your leadership. I may discover that folks are stealing from the company or breaking the law. I feel there is only one way to stop that: to present such issues to law enforcement and to recover every possible nickel, because that is money your employees have earned." From that day on, I had outstanding support not only from this chairman but also from all of his direct reports. Even with good intentions, however, this does not always happen.

In some corporate cultures, it takes time to understand the internal politics and pressures that will be applied to you as a security leader. Even if the manager or executive who was hiring you was open and clear, you usually don't fully absorb how situations will impact you until you experience them. Such risk is implicit in most careers where you end up in a senior leadership role.

Giving you a true latitude to lead may be more than an executive has envisioned or expected. Some business leaders merely want a subordinate who will manage the details and recurring problems of security. While issue and problem management are always a part of the job, exerting a truly positive impact on the organization means analyzing the *status quo* in a number of security areas and then stepping up to initiate positive changes. In Company Five, I stepped into a situation in which the horses were out of the barn, the barn had burnt to the ground, and now they wanted the horses back.

For example, I discovered in one organization that HR had been investigating an employee for over 3 years because the employee had made specific threats to harm some of his coworkers. Over a 100 employees had been scared to death during this time, and there was a lot of back and forth between HR and labor attorneys and uncertainty about what to do. None of this was known to anyone in corporate security.

This serious and unresolved threat was the result of letting internal company politics dictate how the organization dealt with serious issues. Simply put, the head of HR had continually turned a blind eye to the efforts by anyone outside the HR department to be involved and that was the leader's position in spite of past successes in other HR environments. We knew how to be effective across many corporate functions and had developed the trust and support among all senior leaders which consistently yielded good solid results. In Company Five, I found out I had a whole new set of lessons to learn. At the time I viewed this as another opportunity to build clear expectations around security's role and responsibilities and make HR more effective.

My task sounded simple. It was to develop a security program that was consistent across the business and compliant with industry regulations and standards. Some of these were voluntary, others were mandatory. All needed to be verifiable on a routine basis. I had no idea what a huge undertaking this would be.

I wanted to design and implement a comprehensive security vision with goals that truly meant something to everyone, from the Board of Directors to first-line managers. The challenge was to remove security issues from the in-boxes of management at every level of the organization. In a large business, this can seem overwhelming. And it is, if you do not have the right leadership with the right processes.

In Company Five, no one involved in security had ever taken that kind of approach. As a result there was a huge backlog of security issues that were never properly addressed or resolved. These kinds of problems never seem to just go away in spite of good intentions. Complications routinely return, requiring more of management's time and energy, and adding to frustration and loss of credibility.

I had transitioned from companies with collaborative, inclusive cultures to one where decisions were made from the top down. In some cases, there was not only a lack of cooperation but also important segments of the business confused about basic issues of HRs, law, and professional communication. Having had the experience of well-functioning staff that are integral to a business, I was now faced with a variety of organizational dysfunctions in Company Five. After months of travel to get an overview of the business, I realized in disbelief that I was not dealing with isolated organizational issues, but with systemic problems across the entire enterprise.

Building sustainable security systems in such a culture triples the effort, but I was committed to doing so. One challenge was to control my temper and not allow the company's internal competing forces to be turned against both my business and security goals.

As my observations crystallized, I met with senior executives and shared my conclusions:

- The environmental health and safety department was the only area employing consistent processes.
- All other aspects of the business—HR, information technology (IT), corporate communications, regulatory, legal, ethical compliance, auditing, and finance—were using multiple and inconsistent processes.
- Inconsistencies leave the door open for security violations. On the other hand, departments that function intelligently and collaboratively deliver business results. Security functions need to be integrated with every department in order to contribute to the bottom line.
- Because of the nature of the energy business, this company desperately needed a solid security program.
- In order to succeed in the task for which I had been hired, I needed to establish good relationships with all the operational leaders.
- I also needed to recruit a small core security team that could mitigate and resolve the company's security challenges to deliver solid business results.
- Finally, the security program must be built for long-term sustainability across the business.

I knew I had thrown down the gauntlet. As I crisscrossed the various businesses and functions of Company Five in the 7 months of travel and analysis, I saw clearly that the process across this Company was—there is no process. Even corporate communications had three loosely connected functions that sent different messages to both employees and customers. Processes as simple as conducting employee background investigations turned out to be routinely inconsistent. Over time and with additional mergers and acquisitions, these differences compounded Company Five's problems and financial outcomes.

This meeting seemed to get the attention of executives. I continued working. Over the next 11 months I designed a core security program in conjunction with senior leaders in major segments of the business that would deliver meaningful security to employees and to their business operations. The program was structured around a lean staff of three professionals and one administrative position I had requested 7 months into the job. This staff would focus on fulfilling the security needs that the senior business leaders had acknowledged were paramount to their operations.

However, during this same period, the first 18 months of my employment in Company Five, it had undergone two major reorganizations and according to rumor, a third was imminent. The next reorganization took place. I was asked to wait on hiring a security team. The longer we waited the busier things became; two of us were interacting with 8,000 employees in 15 states. The new structure and strategy for security absolutely required two additional security professionals. We waited and waited.

Meanwhile, we dealt with security regulations from a variety of federal and state agencies, handled serious workplace violence issues, and multitasked constantly. In the end, after the new security plan was approved, I waited exactly 1 year to begin implementing it.

I requested a second executive meeting and indicated that it was time for me to make a transition out of Company Five. I had simply gotten nowhere in the past year. As I put it, I didn't know if they didn't trust me or thought I didn't know what I was talking about, but it had become apparent that security was not the priority I had been previously told it was. I decided that it was professionally irresponsible for me to continue as their security leader. From a personal standpoint, I was not about to let my reputation of over 30 years be sullied because management failed to act.

I handed my boss a written summary of what had been promised 18 months earlier as well as the major issues still facing the operations across the corporation. He read the summary and agreed that I had been hired to do a job and that Company Five's leadership had not delivered. All I wanted was to put my experience, skills, and knowledge at the service of the employees and the enterprise. But I was finished waiting. I knew delay could endanger not only the prosperity of the business but also the lives as well.

Within 60 days we had added two excellent members to our security team. Two months later the entire program was up and running.

Although I felt the weariness of a long-distance runner, I was glad I had stood my ground. I share this story so that you too are prepared to hold fast to your core values. If you don't care about people, it is likely to be hard to be a successful security leader. When I completed my work at Company Five, they had a sustainable security program. I was ready to march on and to the beat of my own drum.

CHAPTER 2

A New Road Beckons

Some things are very personal. A person's background, experience, skills, and values are interwoven into every decision he or she makes, especially in undertaking a major life transition. I have just shared my professional itinerary with you to give you an overview of the kinds of things that can happen, even in well-planned transitions. Now I will address the general transition from any form of government or military service to joining the business world, especially as a security leader. In Chapter 3, I will discuss how to explore more specific questions, what you should consider before signing on as security leader of a company. Each of us learns as we go. It is partly because I have made some transitions with ease and others with difficulty that I have something to share with you.

Every aspect of my Marine Corps and DEA service has been a building block for success in corporate America. I owe much of what I have learned to the discipline of the Corps as well as to the challenges of the drug wars. Along the way, I have emulated those I admire. I have drawn on experiences of family, the Marines, and the DEA to build strong, meaningful, and functional relationships with individuals and teams. As I have matured, core values have become clearer; I try to live by them.

Many who became civil servants in their 20s chose to persevere for 20 years for several reasons, including reliable retirement with benefits. As they rose in the ranks, they oversaw a staff and they delivered routine outcomes well. In business, by contrast, those who hire are looking not for routine fulfillment of duty, but for creativity, drive, and problem-solving abilities.

Anyone transitioning from one career to another faces many unknowns. If you are about to move from a highly structured law enforcement or military organization where you are well known, and where you have grown professionally, perhaps you make certain assumptions. Let us explore these.

Each branch of the military—army, air force, coast guard, marines, and navy—has its own culture. There are also various traditions and ways of thinking characteristic of federal agencies: think of the Bureau of Alcohol, Tobacco, Firearms, and Explosives (ATF), Drug Enforcement Administration (DEA), Federal Bureau of Investigation (FBI), Immigration and Customs Enforcement (ICE), and the US Secret Service (USSS). Or consider the cultures of large police departments, such as Los Angeles, Chicago, New York, or Boston.

Those who have been successful in military and law-enforcement careers share certain commonalities such as:

- They work hard on the job and take advantage of educational and professional opportunities.
- They enjoy structured environments.
- They fit into the culture of their organization.
- Ordinarily, they have strong mentors early in their career.

Many of us have known peers who struggled personally and professionally in government service because one of the above factors was missing. We recall some who struggled just to make it to retirement and others who left after a few years.

Now you are considering moving into the world of business where the culture and expectations are very different from those you have known. Eager, talented, and knowledgeable public-sector professionals struggle to effectively transform their prior experience and themselves as they move into the world of entrepreneurs. Persons who make this change without ever having connected with a business find the transition especially challenging. In order to succeed and be happy as a security leader, you must realize that you are hired to deliver business results within a security framework. Are you envisioning your task in this light?

Building supportive relationships is an important aspect of success in any environment. Some people do this naturally; they seem to have an endless spectrum of contacts with individuals from all walks of life, as well as with business, community, and professional associations, educational and faith-based institutions, and other groups. Their relationships provide them with broad access to resources that can help them to address many problems.

Sometimes those who have had successful careers in traditional law enforcement, intelligence, or the military take work relationships for granted. Maintaining solid professional contacts on a military base or in government ranks is relatively easy. People tend to form close bonds with at least some coworkers, and these relationships become a key to their success. Some produce great results year after year, with few setbacks. Those who achieve high rank in these highly-structured organizations typically come to enjoy automatic access to superiors; they have impact across their organization. If this describes you, be prepared for big changes if you choose private sector employment.

You will need to tap into an extensive personal network, as well as a professional network of security executives. This is a two-way street. If you extend yourself to help others, and make an investment in people, they have a way of returning the favor when you need their advice and support. Challenging environments call you beyond yourself; they require a team approach. Moreover, your informal team will grow exponentially over time.

If you want to be part of the next generation of security leaders, it is essential that you seek out security practitioners who have successfully made the leap from public to private sector. Also, the security profession has many outstanding organizations with a wide range of resources to help you along the way. Make use of them. If you are stepping into a national or global security role, you will be presented with challenges you never anticipated. This is normal.

We all need to have networks of security colleagues as well as personal resources to help balance our perspectives. Tap into organizations that have local, national, and global resources: ASIS International, ISMA (International Security Management Association), CSI (Computer Security Institute), the ACFE (Association of Certified Fraud Examiners), and the SEC (Security Executive Council).

These professional organizations have helped transform almost every aspect of security and its leaders. Their magazines, publications, and web sites enable security officers to network as well as to develop mature skills. Other business professional organizations in accounting, human resources, engineering, sales, and facilities management were founded decades ago. Some financial professional groups were established in the nineteenth century. Security is a new member of the business family. In contributing to the success of a large corporation, it is now as necessary as any other department.

The security colleagues you meet in professional organizations will be involved in a variety of industries and understand a wide range of security disciplines. They include persons in and out of government. Many of us have found others who will freely lend their assistance and networks both domestically and internationally as the need arises. Having such a network that can be called upon 24/7 in cases of urgent need is a distinguishing mark of excellent security leaders. Professionals use their networks to build outstanding teams and programs and they willingly share the breadth of their resources. Don't be a lone wolf. Be confident enough in your ability not to try to do everything by yourself. Being open to coaching from others brings both professional balance and strength.

I have frequently asked successful colleagues the secret of their accomplishments in security leadership. Most attribute their achievements to:

- Belonging to an excellent company with sensible communications and organization
- Taking advantage of every opportunity that presents itself to help the company reach its goals
- Using creative approaches to apply security skills to help the business, its employees and executives succeed
- Having an extensive network to call on for problem solving.

These are among the keys to success for business security leaders.

Leaders in government, and sometimes in business, assume that senior public-sector command personnel have the knowledge, skills, abilities, and relationships to lead security initiatives in a civilian agency. They may further assume that a government career has prepared such a person to lead corporate security in a large Fortune 500 Company. These are sometimes risky assumptions.

Before undertaking a transition, you need to understand how businesses work. To refresh your business concepts, I recommend that you read *What the CEO Wants You to Know* by Ram Charan. This book of less than 150 pages is an excellent primer on business basics. It also provides a clear understanding of how companies large and small function and deliver results.

Business profitability is the goal. Although this may be a new framework for those who come to security from public service, corporations offer unique opportunities to address security issues in ways not previously understood in either government or in the business you join. Are you a person who enjoys such challenges and sees them as an adventure of both learning and service?

Be prepared to assess the current state of security across the company you join. As a new security leader, here are some questions you may wish to consider:

- Is there a process to report thefts of money, property, and other losses? Where does this information go? Get copies of theft reports for the last 3–5 years and request copies of all future reports.
- Is any area in the business involved in investigations—functions such as HR, Ethics, Operations, IT, etc., doing background, workplace violence, ethics, inappropriate use of IT or other asset loss investigations, etc.?
  - Determine to whom they report. Are personnel appropriately trained to perform such investigations?
  - Is their training current and does it meet the needs of the business?
- Are there any special security-compliance regulations, requirements, or laws that impact the business?
  - If so, who monitors them—HR, legal, etc.
  - Who is accountable to ensure appropriate follow-up actions for the business?
- Does the business have other special security requirements based on any of its core business operations?
  - Is the business part of the national infrastructure, does it conduct highly confidential research, or have special contracts with the military, etc.?
- Are there any security contracts that the business currently has for guard services, access control, investigations of any type, CCTV, IT security systems, etc.?
  - If so, get copies of these and any similar contracts that have a security nexus.
  - Is there any history of threats to employees, operations, or of workplace violence in any part of the business? Does the business have foreign operations in high threat areas of the world?
    - If so, who knows the history of such incidents or has copies of previous assessments or investigations?

- What is the level of security awareness across the general employee population?
  - If there are existing security personnel, either proprietary or contract, what is their level of security training?
  - Is there a meaningful security component addressing the businesses supply change management program?
  - Is this security component aligned with all supply chain management contracts with third party and their downstream suppliers?

Information or answers to the above questions will give a new security leader a good general sense of past security practices. It will also provide a historical understanding of issues that the business has dealt with.

However, do not assume such a review will give the security leader a comprehensive understanding of what the business *should* be dealing with. The information is likely to be fragmented, overlapping, and hard to get. In one of the companies I joined it took months to get the outsourced security contracts from the corporate contracting office located on the other side of the building.

When I finally got the contracts I could see why employees were dragging their feet. Most contracts had been extended year after year with absolutely no effective review. In addition, the increases requested by the vendors, which averaged around 3% per year, were always approved. These increases alone had cost the operating units an additional 30% in overhead during those 10 years and with lousy performance at that.

You may never get it for a variety of reasons, including internal resistance to providing it. Such obstructions tell you something about the organization. Does it have sound internal discipline and processes or not? Your best chance of making an impact in such an organization comes from working initially with departments that have sensible processes in place. Are you interested in ferreting out information such as that listed above? Are you persistent enough to go after it, in a way that identifies for you who are your allies? Are you willing to work with such people as part of your extended team?

Many of our colleagues who have moved from public service into the private sector realize that businesses—especially large, multinational ones—are sometimes much more bureaucratic than many government operations. The point here is for the potential security leader to get a reasonable sense of both the short- and long-term security issues you will face and the processes—or lack thereof—through which the business has attempted to address problems prior to your arrival. Are you willing to sort out bureaucratic tangles?

In business, you are being evaluated through the eyes and ears of every manager you meet. News about your performance travels fast at the water cooler and through the grapevine. In public service when you arrived at a new office, or new command, you had the respect of your peers. You are an heir, in military or government service, to a long history of a well-defined culture. In business this is not necessarily the case. You will need to introduce yourself. Be ready to tell your story in a way that will entertain, inform, and engage your coworkers.

Listen well too. We were given one mouth and two ears for a reason. Encourage your coworkers to talk about themselves. Where did they grow up, go to school, get the most professional experience and why? Toward the end of every conversation, it may be valuable to get the person's impressions of security and what it does or doesn't do for their operations. Notice, I did not say what it does for the larger corporation. You have a lot to share about your history. Are you willing to work on selling yourself in this new environment?

How you share your experiences and expectations is worth the investment of considerable time and effort. Among the most important selling opportunities is what some call a 30-second elevator response to "who are you and what do you do here?" At one company I had it down to "I am the director of security and I am here to enhance the safe, secure delivery of our energy resources to our customers. What do you do?" Then just wait, you will find you get follow-up questions. Besides the 30-second commercial you will need to have a variety of stories you can tell. Are you willing to prepare them?

The 2007 book, *Whoever Tells the Best Story WINS* by Annette Simmons, goes into detail about how to increase your success in business through the use of stories. She provides a clear and simple structure, explaining how important it is to express yourself in stories to enhance your overall effectiveness in the business. Annette has wonderful sections on:

- Who-I-Am Stories
- Teaching Stories
- Vision Stories

- Values-in-Action Stories
- I-Know-What-You-Are-Thinking Stories.

Many successful security leaders have used stories to communicate effectively throughout their careers. Unfortunately, many more have never understood which ones to share and which ones never to divulge. Let me assure you it will be money and time well spent reading Annette Simmons' book.

The story approach is one that relates who you are, what you have done, and what you can do for the organization. The best-developed stories highlight how you, as a security leader, can facilitate your organization's goals and enhance security while also driving profitability. Why should you be concerned about telling your story?

In the business world the leaders who hired you won't understand what you can do for them—or their business operations—until they see that in fact you are delivering bottom-line results. They will be polite and they will listen to your ideas. However, you are only going to get real buy-in when you first successfully resolve a difficult issue, a workplace violence event, a fraud, a theft, an embezzlement, or a rescue of employees from some part of the world that is in utter chaos.

All they will know is that you are the new security leader. Having a half dozen or so stories of success in your previous organization—explained in business terms through what I refer to as corporate speak—will enable them to better understand how you may be of value in helping them solve problems in their business operations.

One of the early hurdles you may face in adjusting to your new environment is an attitude that "those in government are a bunch of bureaucrats who don't know much." Those of us who have public/private sector experience know that this is not always so. Some businesses are chaotic. Even multimillion dollar companies may have extremely wasteful procedures, or lack thereof. For example, one company had outsourced its finance operations to a contractor who subcontracted them to a third organization in Brazil. Tracking business expenses was impossible. The inefficiencies and frustrations that developed from this arrangement landed employee morale in the dumpster.

Another challenge: although much has changed since 9/11, you may come across corporate myths about security. You will need to tactfully dismantle these over time. For example, until the late 1990s, security might be located in any part of the business. Security leaders were often retired law enforcement personnel; the image of their work was connected with the corporate cop and the accompanying myth was that security consisted of guns, gates, and guards.

Typically, corporate security personnel reported to middle managers three or six levels down in the organization. Often, the only time the head of security met with any senior leader was when something had gone terribly wrong; more usually this person was tapped as a corporate driver, or was asked to get trespassers out of the boss's parking place. Security budgets paralleled those for cafeteria, grounds maintenance, and custodial contracts. Security contracts were often outsourced, and based on the lowest bid. Training was not usually part of the budget; if it were, it could only be accessed locally. There was no security awareness training for employees. The task of the leader for many years was like that of "Guy Noir, Private Eye"—wait until the phone rings.

Because of advances in other areas of business, in HR and in marketing, for example, as well as changes such as corporate globalization and the advent of terrorism, security disciplines that protect employees, information, facilities, and brands are now embedded in smart businesses. Security has catapulted from the basement to the executive suite. However, vestiges of older mentalities may remain in very traditional companies. It is wise to be alert for these vestiges and to be ready to bring to corporate leaders a new awareness of ways a lean and smart security team helps drive the business. Are you both capable and willing to do this?

If you are new to business, look for a company whose processes and values are finely tuned to drive efficiency and profits. Designing and developing a consistent, compliant, and verifiable security program in such a business will tap into every aspect of a lifetime of skills derived from your experience; it can be pure joy.

Whether you are being tested, or are being given new opportunities to deliver meaningful security results for an organization, security work carries a unique level of responsibility. As a result, it is full of opportunities to grow personally and professionally.

Sometimes you may be handed an opportunity to make a difference soon after you join a company. One of the advantages of having had a full law enforcement, military or intelligence career is that you know how to deal with surprises. Here was one of mine.

Our HR vice president came to my office saying her business unit had a problem. An employee who was well known in the company was identified as having embezzled funds. It was a big shock to everyone who knew her. After reviewing the information and determining there was a solid criminal case I persuaded the management team, after lengthy discussion, to let me take the case forward to the district attorney for prosecution. I had been candid with management that once we turned our evidence over to law enforcement we were not in the driver's seat.

As evidence mounted, I briefed the top three leaders of the business every 10 days on the status of our case. These briefings gave me private time with these executives without any interruptions, a really good beginning. They relied on my experience regarding how to handle this issue; they came to trust me too. Later on, their trust would prove invaluable as we dealt with even more important security issues.

The confidential manner in which I was able to manage this and other issues quickly opened doors to other senior business leaders to discuss their security concerns. The senior leaders from across the enterprise who had been sitting on the fence with a "wait and see" attitude toward security began asking how we could help them with various problems in their operations.

Once you deliver results executives become your best allies. I was fortunate because these business leaders appreciated the handling of this sensitive matter and gave their support to an entire new vision of security. They realized that security can support good values, help drive company goals, and be proactive in preventing future problems.

You bring gifts as you transition from the public to the private sector. In government or military service, you may have perhaps performed some of the following tasks and grown in the skills of:

- Constructing and overseeing multimillion dollar budgets
- Managing liaison with local, state, and national law enforcement agencies

- Evaluating organizational performance
- Interviewing potential employees
- Interviewing criminal suspects
- Bridging interservice rivalries
- Conducting audits and inspections
- Dealing with the unexpected in life-threatening situations
- Losing a friend or a colleague on the job, in violent circumstances
- Making quick decisions that may have life or death consequences.

I encourage you to add to this list from your own history. Then consider how you can translate your leadership experiences into business success. Do this in a way that executives can understand and see the value your skills and know-how brings to them as they seek to accomplish their goals. Do that and you will be on the short path to earning their trust. Learning the nuances and rhythms of your new organization will allow you to lead and integrate security in a way that makes the jobs of other executives easier. They will have fewer distractions, interruptions, and see a better bottom line.

Because of your experience, you bring certain advantages to the business world. Tough crises, scenes of violent crime, and life and death decisions test a person's mettle. It takes skill and discipline to testify in court and persistence to follow a case to a successful conclusion. A certain basic willingness to serve also involves discipline. For 14 years, I thought the GS (in GS-1811) stood for "government servant," rather than the more prosaic "general schedule" which has to do with an employee's pay status. To this day, I prefer my first understanding of GS.

Many in public service have held both operations and headquarters positions. The flexibility required to move from one level of service to another develops balance, resilience, and a focus on the needs of the organization, not simply one's own career. For example, in the DEA, I began as a Special Agent working in the New York Division office. Eventually, I was reassigned to headquarters in Washington, DC, and after some years, I became the chief of agent resources.

In this position I was responsible to manage Special Agent recruiting; to select candidates for the DEA Academy; to reassign and promote agents. My peers called me the Job Fairy, although I preferred the title: Duke of Deployment. Later, in Texas, I returned to field work. Moving from the highly charged and frequently changing environment of headquarters, where internal politics can be challenging, back to protecting the lives of agents and others in the field is a valuable exercise.

By contrast, many employees in business have spent entire careers in finance, or sales, or marketing, or human resources, or communications. Their experience tends to be either headquarter-centric or field-centric. This is especially true of middle managers, who may be confined to one department only. Perhaps they are expert at what they do, but their experience can also be self-limiting.

This is especially true when it comes to dealing with serious incidents, or a crisis that crosses multiple functions in the corporation. While you can learn what many of these executives know, they may never have the tested mettle that is yours because of your life history—your path. Therefore, they need you—as long as you are also willing to learn everything you can from them about their business. This becomes a win-win situation if you work hard, look for opportunities to apply security skills within the company's culture, and keep your eye on enhancing the bottom line.

In every organization there will be some who will never see the value you bring. Do not allow them to frustrate you. Once you have given them a fair chance to collaborate, leave them behind, and deal with those leaders and parts of the business that are receptive and responding. This is something like driving down the highway and encountering major construction. It may slow you down, but you don't let it keep you from continuing your journey, unless you develop a bad case of road rage and have an accident. Difficulties come with the security leader's territory; a sense of humor also helps you deal with them effectively.

When someone moves into a new leadership role in business, it is not unusual for them to rely on their subordinates to give them an orientation. If you assume the lead security position in a corporation, you have no such luxury. You will be expected to hit the ground running and get your decisions right the first time.

SEC recently concluded research that highlights key skills that the next generation security leaders need in order to be successful in bringing value to their company's business operations. The following leadership skills are considered essential:

- Communications skills
- Presentation skills
- Project management
- Organizational skills
- Business acumen
- Strategic planning abilities
- Relationship management
- International experience
- Team building
- Negotiation skills
- Decision-making skills
- Cost control management.

Remember, very few of even the most experienced and talented security leaders have every one of the above skills. If you have a good base in most of these skills, along with a focus on building strong teams and a personal and professional network it will help you compensate for skills that are not as strong. But you need both aptitude and flexibility for personally developing the majority of these skills within yourself. Finally, long-term success will be found in your own willingness to hone your developmental opportunities and continually work to strengthen them.

Show up every day. Learn the business. Be honest. Work like hell. If you bring personal discipline, are thoughtful toward others, deliver on the commitments you have made, and introduce humility and fun into your daily work, you will become that next-generation security leader the next generation so desperately needs.

CHAPTER *3*

Reconnaissance (Before You Sign On)

The journey of a thousand miles begins with a single step.

Chinese Proverb

Before you sign on as a security leader with any company, be sure that you have the skills outlined in Chapter 2, or that you are willing to work hard to acquire those you will need as part of a team. In order to do such tasks with competence and eventually with some ease, you must truly enjoy most parts of the job—including the challenges. Once you have realistically assessed your skills, usually in consultation with others—preferably persons who know both you and the field of security leadership—you must not be hesitant to negotiate what is right for you.

Prepare carefully for interviews. For example, research the company and its executives in some of the ways suggested below; reflect on the culture of the company and whether it appeals to you; and be especially alert for any tough questions that occur to you and think about how you want to ask them. Courtesy may seem to be an old-fashioned virtue, but it is much in demand and indicates a level of *savoir-faire*—the know-how needed in security leadership.

When I returned to Syracuse from the Marine Corps, I thought I wanted to be a salesman for a large company. I had interviewed with IBM and some other businesses and had been offered positions, but nothing interested me. My dad encouraged me to apply for work at the company he had served for many years. I met with the president and owner of the firm, laid out what I could do, and what I wanted to be paid. I thought the interview had gone very well; the president, however, was shocked at my forthrightness.

Soon after this interview, I entered federal law enforcement. I was not interviewed again for over 20 years. Since then, I have been in many leadership roles in corporations. What I have learned is, during interviews, be as direct as possible and don't overstate your qualifications. Tell the firm's representatives what you can and cannot do, what you expect of the organization's leaders, your priorities in terms of access to the C-level, and anything else that you see as critical to your serving this company well. Listen carefully and be observant for what this company does in practice, not just what it says about itself.

Honest interviews prevent second guessing later on. You know your tasks for the company and executives know what you expect of them. Such agreements at least get you off on a sound footing.

Successful organizations have a variety of underpinnings. One of the most important of these is professional discipline. This attribute may be evaluated at many levels. From the time you first contact an organization, or they contact you, begin keeping notes. How was the contact initiated? Once an inquiry goes beyond an informal review of your resume, pay particular attention to how those in the business heard of you.

As you research the company formally and informally, as well as during your interviews, be alert for anything that seems out of sync. Try to get perspective on the company from someone who knows both its operations and its culture. Here are some specific questions to consider:

- Is the interview process itself well defined and professionally conducted?
- Is the reception area a controlled environment? Was your arrival anticipated?
- Were employees, executives, and others wearing ID badges?
- Are those who come into the building checked in electronically or visually at points of entry?
- What books, pictures, or artwork decorate the office?
- How are you seated for the interview? Is the atmosphere formal or informal?
- Does the music of peoples' body language harmonize with their words? (At least 80% of communication is nonverbal.)
- Do you feel comfortable, or out of place, in this environment?
- Does anything strike you as too casual or disorganized?
- Are those conducting the interview interested in you personally or only in your qualifications?
- Are questions clear, intuitive, and posed in ways that generate your interest to know more about this opportunity?

- Are interviewers probing your values?
- Are they placing great emphasis on compensation?
- Are your questions answered honestly and without undue defensiveness?
- Has the organization spelled out the responsibilities and accountabilities of the new security leader?
- Is there a formal written job description?
- Is it clear to you what this company needs from you and the time frame in which they expect you to deliver on goals and objectives?
- Are there human resource professionals within the business who will support your work?
- Is the general culture of the company enthusiastically cooperative rather than unhelpful or careless of business outcomes? What makes you think that way? How can you tell?
- Are day-to-day matters handled with an appropriate level of urgency and professionalism?
- Can you assess or determine the measures, metrics, and processes that the business uses?
- What level of liveliness do employees display, especially in areas such as customer service?
- Are existing security team members and others interested in personal and professional growth?
- Have there been numerous mergers or turnovers in key personnel? Have departmental and executive roles been sorted out in the aftermath of changes?
- Are members of the executive team participating in your interview? Can any of them discuss security with the same enthusiasm as they might speak of sales, marketing, finances, or operations? If not, how do you think security will be prioritized among the other functions of the organization?
- Are policies and procedures clear?
- Is there a well-established security function in place or is this a start-up?
- Has the company delivered consistent and smooth business results, year after year?
- How does the company manage internal communications among its employees?
- What important security issues has the company faced within the last 5 years? How have they been resolved?
- How is the morale of operational managers?

- Do people who work for this corporation take good care of their health? Do they have adequate family and vacation time?
- What about teamwork within departments? Are departments collaborative between each other?
- If travel arrangements were needed, were they well coordinated, or is this a new experience for this company?
- Are follow-up contacts timely?
- How do you feel at a gut level about working for this company?

Immediately after the interview, make extensive notes. The more details you recall, the more clearly you will understand how this business addresses processes. These are a clear indicator of the level of organizational discipline throughout the company, as well as of its commitment to employees. If you join this company, you will mirror and adopt their business processes—or you will spend a great deal of energy in frustration.

Become an observer of people—what they do and how they do it. If this is not a natural attribute, you will need to develop it because it will help you to intuitively understand individual and organizational security practices. It will also be a key to grasping changes that may need to be made very quickly if you join this business. Initially, you will be looking for simple win-win opportunities, so note them as you are being interviewed. If the business wins first with suggestions you make, security will automatically win second. This should be your goal.

Also notice anything that strikes you as sluggish or unresponsive; this tends to be mirrored in how security teams and programs respond to challenges. Given the nature of the work and the small size of most corporate security teams, it is not uncommon for any member of the team to be responding to a customer or to the CEO. Therefore, members of the team need to be able to interact appropriately in a variety of situations. Even the most casual interactions reflect the professionalism, or lack thereof, of the security team.

Seek to avoid business environments in which either your lack of certain skills or the culture presents challenges that do not compliment your personal strengths. It is important to identify and build on your natural talents. Doing so makes for a more enjoyable and longer life.

People tend to be happiest with the right amount of challenge—no more, no less. A talented colleague moved from running his own security consulting business back into a major corporation as a high-level manager. He had already been in a similar role with a different global corporation before he began his own business. However, he knew that after being away from the major corporate level, he needed to reenter the profession under the supervision of a senior security executive. Since then, he has had many opportunities to take the top spot, but he realizes the advantages of his current position and the stability it brings to him and his family. I believe he has been very smart about his career choices.

Sometimes, it is wise to forego offers of the top position; many have found value in this and have improved their opportunities for personal growth, as well as long-term professional success. I encourage you to consider only those position descriptions that describe you, your strengths, and your skills. Too many times, I have watched colleagues with excellent backgrounds transition into positions for which they lack skills. They end up losing, and so do their families, and the organizations that hired them. Nothing is more frustrating.

Do your homework before you commit to a new venture. Today, it is possible to use public records to research the history of an executive all the way back to ones' college days. Finding the histories and backgrounds of key leaders is important, as they are the ones you will need to influence. If you know the path they traveled to get where they are, you have a real advantage in communicating with them.

For example, one of my early business leaders came from a family of great achievement, wealth, and status in industry. Educated at a fine university, everyone who worked with him knew who his daddy was. I did my own research. I listened to true insiders who knew this executive personally and professionally. Although he was affluent, at the age of 16, he worked for a summer in a steel mill, sweating in the midst of production in the midst of some coworkers who had never finished high school and others who had experienced run-ins with the law. He learned about hardwork and about treating others as he would want to be treated.

When I met this executive, I was struck by his respect for each individual; his clear focus on carrying out responsibilities until tasks were finished; his personal and professional balance as a human being; his solid values in every realm; and his ability to entrust others with real responsibility. Getting to know this leader was an important factor in my decision to join his enterprise.

For publicly-traded firms, it will also help your assessment if you can access operating plans, annual reports, and 10-K report for the previous two or three years. Try to grasp both the history and the culture of the organization, especially what has led it to thrive. Here are some other key points:

- Learn as much as possible about those to whom you will report, as well as those who will report to you. Start with raw data that can be found in Google searches and launch out from there.
- Do top executives trust others to lead within their departments? In business, trust is related to the level of direct access you are offered to other executives, and to the scope of responsibility and authority they give you.
- If you join this enterprise, who will be in your corner? This question addresses not only your formal title in the business—vice president, director, etc.—but the titles of those to whom you will report. In general, the higher the executive to whom you report, the more organizational attention and impact you will generate. I have been most successful when I reported to a C-suite executive such as a general counsel or executive vice president for human resources, and when I also had direct access to the chairman and CEO. Strive to report at these levels. Having such relationships open lines of communication which are invaluable, especially if there are layers of operational executives.
- Will leaders let you lead or do they merely want you to manage? I have never joined a group, an agency, an organization, or a business just to manage it. That is not my strength. Although I have managed projects, budgets, activities, investigations, I see management as only one component of leadership. This is an important distinction. By the way, corporations also need good managers. Just be sure you know who you are and convey this in your communication.
- Probably the most challenging business environment for a security leader is one in which the organization has never fully integrated itself. This may apply to staff, operational functions, or both. Nonintegrated structures might work in some environments such as holding companies. However, in traditional top-down companies, or

in those with national or international infrastructures, lack of integration can be disastrous.

- Corporate cultures are diverse; each has its own sense of values. Can you spell out the values that are essential to your personal integrity? How do you live these values in your daily work?
- Does the corporation you are thinking of joining spell out its values? If so, how have they become part of the daily operation of the company? Are there ways in which the company evaluates itself behaviorally on specific criteria? Look for criteria having to do with values and people as well as with finances.
- Is there a solid match between your values and those of the corporation? Your success in an organization depends on the compatibility of your values as they are lived out. Although this sounds simple, sometimes people give years of their lives only to leave disheartened and beaten down. A business environment that does not fit your core beliefs is a career and sometimes a personal killer. It literally can suck the lifeblood out of even the most committed professional.

As you interview, try to get a sense of:

- What won't work for you.
- What may work if the circumstances are well defined and understood up-front.
- What are the aspects of this opportunity that you expect will work for you.

In the match between you and any opportunity:

- What does the organization do, day in and day out, in regard to security?
  - Do not look simply at ethics, values, policies, and procedures statements. If possible make it a point to talk to employees when you are away from those you are meeting with.
  - Look at behaviors and practices—what they do and how they treat employees and other issues on a daily basis.
- Finally, what about your own temperament? Can you be calm in critical situations? Are you willing to put in very long days, and could you do it for say 12–18 months?

The investment in time and energy that you make as you thoroughly explore a company and its leaders before committing to employment will pay dividends every day of your working life. The questions and reflections in this chapter along with your own research, conversations with trusted mentors, journaling, and quiet reflection should help you to make a thorough reconnaissance of the territory you are entering. If the journey of a thousand miles begins with a single step, the steps you are taking now are among the most significant of your entire journey. These steps may set your direction for years to come.

CHAPTER 4

Walking the Trail (After You Sign On)

Without a vision, the people perish.

Prophet Habbakuk, Hebrew Scriptures

Even if you have done your homework well, joining a company is an act of faith—on your part and on the part of those who have newly hired you. Creating a security program from the ground up in a global corporation is one of the most challenging and fulfilling opportunities any security leader can ever experience. If you are fortunate enough to be a member of a senior leadership team in a company that has great values, you will probably find it fun, frustrating, demanding, exhausting, and the source of both personal and professional relationships that will last a lifetime.

In this chapter, I will provide a context for what follows, an orientation to the trail we will be walking together, the trail a person follows to learn a business. Sometimes, this will involve slogging through the mud, as you accompany folks whose tasks are physically difficult, dangerous, and often somewhat taken for granted. At other moments, you will share the big picture with your companions who lead the entire company. And at still others, it may feel that you are walking alone, that you need to find both guides and close companions on your journey.

As your guide, I invite you to sit back as we hit the trail as I map out some of the roads we will travel. The purpose is to help you to be just a little bit better prepared for some of the challenges and opportunities you will encounter on this journey of learning a business and discovering how to integrate security into every aspect of it over time and as a new member of a business team.

Don't let your role as security leader be defined by a position described on paper; rather, make the security leader's position relevant and clear to your colleagues. Putting names with faces and learning about the work of others is a first step in building rapport with your internal business clients. If possible, schedule initial meetings with key executives during your first few days. First impressions are often a good barometer for future dealings.

There is a pragmatic reason for getting to know the leaders of the business early in your employment. You never can control the timing of a serious incident. In the event of a crisis that you may be called upon to manage, at least you will know the names and faces of those who will rely on you. Times spent with executives in relaxed environments can be valuable; make the most of opportunities for one-on-one contact. Know too that others are assessing you constantly.

A security program built synergistically on existing conduits of communication, leveraging existing functional resources, sends a very strong message to executives. They see you as creative, thrifty, and stepping out to learn the business. Another positive aspect of inviting business peers to join your security initiatives is that you are getting to know one another in normal daily business situations.

This really pays off in the event of a major incident, for example, a shooting, a fire at a major facility, an embezzlement that becomes public in the media, or the loss of international travelers in a terrorist event.

Working together in normal environments develops confidence over time. When a major event occurs, the time you have invested in getting to know leaders and coworkers pays enormous dividends. I encourage you to be candid with your business colleagues. Tell them you are committed to learning from them. Take a sincere interest in their personal backgrounds as well as in their professional perspectives and career experience. Demonstrating openness gives them the opportunity to reciprocate and learn about your skill set and your vision.

In addition to getting to know the key individuals, it is important to keep the big picture in view—something like the map showing where you are now, as well as your destination. The security executive's role is to mitigate a broad spectrum of security-related risks to the business. Doing so requires you to know the factual security issues the business faces. Seeing how the company operates, and what it does to make a profit, is essential to increase your business acumen.

You require a thorough understanding of how various areas work to deliver value to the company, as well as how they interact with each other. Such hands-on learning results in a positive impact on safety and security issues and delivers measurable business results. This can be a difficult and long task.

Learning the real infrastructure of any large company is challenging, because you are gradually digging down into the cultural roots of the organization. If the company has grown by acquisition or a series of acquisitions you are like an archaeologist, coming across the deep strata of multiple cultures. Do not be surprised if, initially, some employees and mid-level leaders do not have time for you or for one another. They may be too busy multitasking and keeping their heads down to avoid the next reorganization.

Make note of this. In business today, the level of multitasking is taking its toll on employees, supervisors, and managers alike. Many are simply overwhelmed; they are "siloed" in their own processes at the business units they run. It is important to approach some issues judiciously and in some cases with empathy. Oft times, company functions that are not well integrated have employees frequently multitasking and have so much to do that they may not be able to see the forest for the trees.

On your initial journeys across the business, you will be crossing into the jurisdictions of other more established departments. Be prepared for some in the workforce to view your visit, message, and intent with an attitude just short of hostility. It is natural for people to protect their turf until you win their trust by demonstrating that you are there to make their work safer, easier, and more productive for them and the business.

You should be encouraged to visit the following departments, and perhaps others, given the nature of the business:

- Audit/Finance
- Business Development (mergers and acquisitions)
- Human Resources
- Information Technology
- Facilities Management
- Ethics/Compliance
- Environmental Health/Safety
- And all key business operations and segments.

After visiting even a few of the above departments, you will probably begin to see gaps in the security structure of the company. Such
gaps, if unaddressed over time, leave the company extremely vulnera-
ble in ways that even seasoned executives may not realize.

The protection of employees and contractors, as well as business
processes, facilities, brands tied to the identity of the business, and various kinds of information and systems, including IT, is initially confusing, and, in a large corporation, always complicated. This is especially
true if departments are competing with one another for company
resources.

Your task as a security leader is something akin to aligning the col-
ors of a Rubik's Cube, an excellent symbol of the complexities of integrating security functions into highly regulated industries such as those
dealing with chemicals and energy. After 26 years in public service and
a couple of very successful corporate experiences I thought I knew
something about government regulations and their impact on business.
I was in for a whole new education when I came face to face with the
multiplicity of federal and state law enforcement agencies that regulate
these infrastructures.

At one company, there were 9 federal and 36 state agencies (four
per state) for a total of 45 government entities that had some sort of
security jurisdiction over its operations. Moreover, at any given time,
any one of these bodies could significantly impact our business. By the
way, no one in this company had been monitoring pending security
legislation at the federal or state legislatures in whose jurisdictions we
had substantial business operations. A Rubik's Cube indeed!

It is usually wise not to comment on your observations until you
have a sufficiently clear overview to know the company's culture first-
hand, as well as your priorities for establishing an integrated security
function across the business. You may receive requests for feedback
from those you are visiting about, what you think about their
approach to security, or how you see their challenges, for example.

Apart from noting something that poses a truly immediate danger,
or presents a glaringly obvious vulnerability, resist the temptation to
comment. The functional and operational leaders who have owned
chunks of security for their area will profess to "want to help you"

when they may actually only be interested in whether your findings have uncovered problems in their department or business operations.

I frequently encountered questions such as: "Well, David, you have seen our operations. What do you think about our security?" Often, individuals responsible for security in that component of the business were present and were very eager to hear my observations. They knew I would provide some kind of feedback to senior management; they had arranged my visit, wined, and dined me; they wanted a quick reaction. In trying to respond immediately to such implicit demands, new security leaders often make mistakes.

Know the business and its culture before making substantive recommendations. The higher up you go on the organization, the more focused your recommendations must be. When the time and place is right, articulate smart business reasons for every aspect of security you intend to challenge or change. Success is all about how you make change—using an intelligent management model that is practical, improves profits, minimizes risks, and creates opportunities for the business.

I am not implying that you need to be secretive or evasive. Simply be clear about your task. At this point, you are merely trying to get a broad picture of security across the organization. Any information you share prematurely will put you into a tactical role that you are not yet ready to play, especially because you are still unearthing the culture or cultures of the corporation.

As you do this initial assessment, you will be working with key leaders of the organization for the first time. If you take a disciplined approach and adhere to your task, this will send a positive message about your professionalism and especially about the confidential nature of the information you are gathering and receiving from those who are open with you.

My good friend and security colleague David Gibbs once wisely advised me that the time of assessment may be a good moment to bring in an outside professional security consultant. If you choose the consultant wisely, you will receive not only a report on existing security issues but also likely a complete new charter, mission, or set of goals for your department. Other business departments like finance,

HR, IT, and environmental safety frequently use outside consultants, so why not security?

Before walking the trail to explore the organization and its various business components, consider some of the areas below as you prepare to hit the road across the business:

- Be brutally honest about your own abilities, knowledge, skills, and deficits. Many mentors have wisely encouraged this from the outset. They have lived the adage that sometimes the truth hurts, but honesty is the only way to deal with serious or life-threatening issues, in business as in any other aspect of walking the walk.
- Insist that you and those on your security team have the same level of honesty and clarity when dealing with the safety and security of the business. Whether in government or the private sector, most of us have the good fortune to work with other great leaders. Such persons will stand their ground and provide appropriate guidance for others. They realize that sometimes, such guidance is the only thing that will keep others out of harm's way.
- Look for security successes that are practical, quick, and smart for the business. You have been hired to produce a positive impact for the business. Business is not looking for knee-jerk reactions or solutions that are as thin as the paper they are printed on. Likewise, do not slash the standing security organization without understanding it. On the other hand, do not bring in an automatic agenda of big-buck technology. Rather, begin moderately by looking for areas that may be draining the bottom line: theft, inefficient use of security resources, waste of time due to responsibilities not being understood or are unclear, etc.
- Realize that you are on a business team. Like other senior leaders—Operations, HR, Legal, Marketing, Sales, etc.—you are also there to drive business results. Show up every day. This really means "be all there" with every bit of you focused on contributing your best. Care about those with whom you work and treat them as you want to be treated. Learn the business from top to bottom. Be honest. Keep any eye on the bottom line. And work hard, because you love making a contribution. These behaviors are basic. These are solid foundations of every successful business.

I cannot say this more directly. You have to learn the business in the mud and be willing to get your hands dirty. Initially, this requires a generous time commitment. Usually it also involves extended travel, which can be exhausting, both physically and mentally. Early breakfast meetings and late dinner meetings are the norm, followed by catching up with e-mail afterward. Expect to put in 12–14 h days. Otherwise, you are not really walking the trail—you are taking a bus.

It is not unusual, once the security leader's position is filled, for the other senior leaders who championed bringing you on board to disappear from view. Some executives simply move on to other pressing issues. Even if you feel somewhat abandoned, do not let this distract you. Effective corporate executives expect those they bring into the organization to be proactive and to blaze their own trails.

My paramount experience of being oriented into a company involved the executives extending themselves and taking five actions:

1. They invited me to key executive business meetings.
2. They asked me to travel with them via the corporate jet to learn the business.
3. They were available and engaged me to find out about what security issues were negatively impacting our employees as well as business goals.
4. They allowed me to lead and expected me to responsibly provide them guidance and options regarding security matters.
5. Finally, they gave me the authority to align our security vision and mission across all segments of the business.

CHAPTER 5

Learning the Business

In order to walk, a person puts one foot in front of the other; every step requires moving from imbalance to balance. It is only by taking this risk that one moves forward.

Anonymous

This chapter builds on the territory we have already covered; you are determined to make a transition; you have done everything in your power to consider if you truly wish to do so; you have tried, with others you trust, to envision the path on which you will embark. Now it is time to hit the trail and to set out on the actual journey. In this journey, you will learn to understand the company you have joined in order to integrate security into every aspect of its operations, so that the business will be more profitable and employees more safe. As you walk the trail, you will be learning new things every day—about yourself, others, and the trail itself. Be open to this hands-on education. Enjoy the trip! Here are some specifics that I have learned by traveling the road. Be alert also to your original learnings. You may choose to keep a journal to make note of them.

5.1 LESSON #1: BE PREPARED TO MOVE THROUGH OBSTACLES

As you hit the trail and begin learning the business, you may find that many mid-level operational leaders across the organization have been dealing with a whole spectrum of security issues. The vast majority of these employees only deal with security because they cannot avoid it. There are some who avoid security tasks for a variety of negative factors:

- Security is a nuisance.
- Security is all about costs.
- Issues such as workplace violence are time consuming.
- Issues such as fraud, theft, or inventory diversion may reflect poorly on their management abilities, and therefore they avoid effectively reporting them.

Some departments are content to handle new employee background screening, hand out ID badges, or approve access to different levels of the company's or customer data. Departments may have developed distinctly different or even conflicting policies, procedures, and practices in resolving identical security issues. HR processes, IT platforms, financial systems, or even a consistent ID badge process may never have been reviewed for the impact it may have across the organization. Because many companies grow through mergers and acquisitions, it is common to find that no one has stepped back to consider the precise needs for security across the entire business enterprise.

As you begin to walk the trail, be prepared for this: some managers will take time for you, while others will call only when there is a significant problem. Sometimes it takes persistence just to make an appointment. Do not consider this a personal affront. Think of it as an opportunity for you to shape what you want to do: drive an effective security agenda, and help keep employees and company assets safe and secure.

5.2 LESSON #2: SIMPLIFY THE JOBS OF YOUR COWORKERS

Offer to take security-related problems off the desks of operational managers and free them to do what they do best: focus on their business goals and responsibilities. Security today is partly a matter of being in compliance with myriads of complex federal, state, and industry regulations or voluntary guidelines. Taking a piecemeal approach to this function is not only a recipe for failure but also a time-consuming distraction for middle managers who have no expertise in this area.

In addition, in today's highly matrixed corporations, staff functions such as HR, environmental safety, and audit tend to add work to the already overloaded desks of operational managers. It is wise for the security leader to do just the opposite, that is, not to dictate how "they" are to handle security issues but to listen to them, understand their challenging work environment, and ultimately make it easier for them to respond and manage workplace violence, theft, and regulation compliance issues that involve security. The real issue is building a security program that is both robust yet truly simple.

For any such program to succeed, you must be brilliant on the basics. You must know the business as it really is in order to deal with its problems. Everything you do as the security leader—and eventually as a member of the security team—must be effective and designed to deliver timely and meaningful business results.

Design your security program to respond to real issues faced by operational managers; do this in collaboration with them. This means acquiring from folks on the ground a sound understanding of threats to employees and to the core segments of the business.

The greatest success of security teams that I led was consistently with old-timers—people who have grown up in a corporation. Most had 15–30 years on the job. They quickly sensed our sincerity when we said that we were focused on helping them deliver better business results with less hassle about security issues; in other words, we were there to serve their needs. I call this approach adaptive security.

Adaptive security initiatives adjust to the needs of both the business and its leaders on all levels. Its programs are based on sound business and security principles. One of the most important aspects of any security initiative is that it be applied in a consistent and meaningful way to benefit customers, employees, and the business itself.

Security basics are outlined in many books, courses, and certification programs. I have found that one of the best texts on essentials is

Rethinking Corporate Security in the Post 9/11 Era by Dennis R. Dalton. I recommend a close reading of this excellent book.

Dalton advocates for three fundamental security units:

1. A unit dedicated to business risk assessment
2. A unit dedicated to employee protection
3. A unit dedicated to mainstream operational support

These elements coalesce only when all significant aspects of the security program can be verified as critical to meeting the goals of the business. I have tailored these three concepts to the hiring of a core team of highly skilled individuals who have diverse business and security skills. I prefer, in the best of all possible worlds, working with a lean and talented team rather than a large one requiring significant supervision. On my team, I want us, together, to master every security skill necessary to meet the needs of a particular business.

The ultimate test of our common work is that we professionally assess business risks; we contribute to the safety and well-being of employees; we support operational leaders in practical ways that are measurable in dollars and cents as well as in employee morale and effective customer service. And we continue to do these tasks on a daily basis. How to build such a team will be discussed in Chapter 8.

5.3 LESSON #3: IDENTIFY YOUR ALLIES

As you walk the trail, you will get to know contractors, engineers, supervisors, managers, and directors. It is these folks who do the daily work, who will tell you what and where the real security issues are. They will tell you what to look for because they see it every day. For example, the only way to learn a facility is to walk it from the inside out and from bottom to top. This means leading by example—literally walking the walk. It requires a willingness to walk the parameter fence lines in winter and to climb to the roof of a million square foot distribution center in 110°F heat to check out what the neighborhood looks like from high over the fences.

This gives you a new perspective on what facility managers are dealing with when intruders gain access or survey your operations to avoid, for example, someone stealing tractor-trailers full of raw materials or finished products. It lets you know how close you are to other industrial sites. It gives you a view of employee parking, entrance, and egress. In addition to this, it gives you solid one-on-one time with the plant manager; it allows you to observe his work style.

In doing this tour, I avoid cell phone and e-mail distractions. I am totally focused on the leader I am with, the management team, and the facility. After all, I am not traveling to get out of the office; I am doing so to learn what security issues the employees, facility, and operational managers are facing, in order to determine how to help them. At the end of each day, I write a one- or two-page summary of my observations. Being well-informed sends a strong message to managers and employees that you are serious about their safety as well as their bottom line.

When you contact managers of a facility to let them know you are coming to visit, prepare a simple message to tell them why you are coming. Here is one that has worked well:

- This is not a security audit. I am visiting to understand your business operations and to make everyone's job easier.
- I want to learn about what you do in order to help you deliver even better business results.
- The way our team does this is by listening to your ideas about how to make the workplace safer and more productive for you, your employees, and your contractors.

Using a process such as this to address security issues has real business value. Assessing the existing security practices of employees in their ordinary work routine is a never-ending task. Usually if I want to know how to "beat" an access control, all I have to do is observe the employees who work in that environment or, once they know they will not get into trouble for telling me, simply ask them how to beat the system.

Eventually, I called the above process SSEaSBP. The Sound Security Expertise and Smart Business Practices are centered on every member of the security team being first and foremost a business partner. Every member of the team must work closely with business leaders at all levels, from corporate vice presidents and general managers to first-line supervisors.

Of equal importance is that each security team member must understand the business plans of those operations they support, as well as whom to engage when dealing with any security matter, be it a simple incident or a crisis.

From the first assessments that are undertaken, we attempt to engage every employee as an ally on the "extended security team." Absolutely nothing counts as much as being a walk-around-security leader as you establish yourself and this approach. You cannot ask others to do it; you must walk the enterprise from executive offices across call centers, onto distribution and manufacturing floors, and into IT data centers. Do not limit yourself to hearing about security concerns from other managers or reading policies and procedures. It is in "walking the walk" that you get to see what is really going on and also will find some genuine allies.

The significance of learning a business came home to me after joining a national infrastructure company that had 90,000 miles of pipes, platforms in the Gulf, compression stations, take points, transmission control operations, and new construction sites. I walked pipelines, ate lunch with transmission and distribution workers, and listened to the guys who made the business systems work from one end to the other.

Employees in the field shared stories of having to work alone doing utility shutoffs for nonpayment of bills in dangerous inner-city neighborhoods, of confrontations and threats posed by marijuana growers in the mountains of Appalachia, and enjoyed describing what it was like to work in the mud doing the day-to-day tasks that kept the company alive. I grew to immensely respect the things they shared about the dangers of repairing old or failed utility lines which are prone to explosion, as well as the unique lifestyles of working on platforms and rigs in the Gulf. I realized that any security program we designed had to support these folks in the field and the unique challenges they faced.

I later discovered that some managers with 20-plus years on the job and who were quick with opinions about what employees were doing had never visited their own field operations, even those within 2 miles of headquarters. Several senior operations and staff members were amazed at the places we had visited.

For me, this reinforced an important lesson. There are sometimes gaps between staff functions and key operations. These gaps lead to breakdowns in communication. Important business processes were not understood. Sometimes, operations were not driving successful business outcomes. Finally, such gaps, either in understanding or communication, leave the security of a corporation riddled with potentially dangerous security gaps. I repeat, it is in walking the walk that you find your truest allies. It is they who will build with you a meaningful security program.

As you get to know those in operational and staff functions, senior- and mid-level managers, be assertive. Invite them to contact you when something goes wrong, long before it begins to spin out of control. Ask them to reach out if they or their employees experience theft, threats, or regulatory compliance issues. Ask them to share with you:

- How much security is just right for you?
- How much security is too much?

The answers to such questions will give you some of your most valuable information that will assist you to shape realistic security programs that meet real needs.

5.4 LESSON #4: IDENTIFY AND VISIT KEY FACILITIES

A key facility is one that is unique in its functions or in its overall importance to the success and sustainability of the business. For example, one business in which I was the security leader had a key facility in the middle of central Missouri. It was the only plant manufacturing a medical device that was both a stand-alone product and a component of several other products that the company made and distributed. The product held a national market share of over 60% and generated a net profit of over 90%. Not bad for a small town in the middle of America.

During our first visit to this facility, we were surprised that security started and ended with the last person out the door turning off the lights and locking the door. The security in place had been the same for as long as anyone could remember. There had never been any kind of security issue or incident. During the day it was common to leave loading dock areas wide open; anyone could enter the facility unobserved. Actually, employees were more concerned about access by small animals rather than people.

While visiting, we discovered that one of the main components in the manufacturing process was nitrates, a main component in making bombs as was used in the Oklahoma City federal building. This fact coupled with national security events led us to recommend and make some changes to security at this facility.

We took our usual approach: listening to the local management team, incorporating their suggestions, and helping them tailor meaningful security measures designed to be easily exercised at their plant. The suggestions of the local employees became part of the facility's overall security plan. After all, they had a vested interest in going home every night and they knew their livelihood was tied to the success of this facility.

Amazingly, in providing a safe, secure environment for the business and its employees, sometimes security can be reconfigured so that ineffective measures are modified or even removed. Cost in many instances may be reduced. Doing this successfully involves listening to and respecting local management and employee input and then taking action. When you start doing that, you find you are taken seriously. Initial skepticism begins to melt away.

As you travel the trail, take note of guard services, access controls, security staffing levels, and other such measures and review them for their cost-effectiveness and appropriateness to today's business. If security measures have been inherited through acquisition or mergers, they may often be trimmed in a judicious way as real security needs are addressed and overall security is improved and always incorporating as much local input as possible. You win, the employees win, and the company wins.

5.5 LESSON # 5: MAKE HASTE SLOWLY

Time and again, security professionals who join new organizations fail to pace themselves. Yet, it is imperative to learn the particular business and its culture before initiating significant changes or business-wide programs. The high turnover rate (corporate speak for being fired) for security leaders who fail to learn the business, and take an autocratic approach, is legendary. "I am the security leader and I know what needs to happen" is a formula for failure. It is costly to the person, to his or her family, to the business itself, and to the security profession as a whole. Frequently such attitudes sour business leaders from considering other public sector leaders with outstanding careers as they seek to transition into the corporate world.

Certainly, a measured approach to building a security program takes longer than rolling out a task of requirements handed down from security. Some executives will begin to question whether they hired the right person to get the job done. The tactical focus of business leaders is often short term; they routinely view security through this lens. They may focus on small and annoying details like someone parking in their space, the ID badge they see no need to wear, can't find, or could care less about using let alone wearing.

So, while a transitioning security leader may see this as being a deliberate leader, the CEO, looking for quarterly results, may see the process as slow or nonproductive. This is the moment for you to be calm and confident in your role. As you develop an understanding of the business, you will certainly start to shape a meaningful vision of security. And if done well, this can have a very positive impact on the bottom line.

At this stage, it is important not to confuse leading with doing. The activity trap can become all consuming; it does not lead to an effective strategy or to good end results. Like other senior leaders, you need perspective to achieve these. In developing your plan for learning the business, consider questions such as these:

- Where are the primary revenue generators (such operations are frequently referred to as "cash cows") in the business?
- What security situations do senior operational leaders worry about?
- What are the work environments like in areas such as customer service, back-office operations, and other areas?
- What are the security concerns of employees?
- What are the significant risks to employees, facilities, or supply chains?

Discover the answers to these questions by listening to the people who do the work, know the business as you visit facilities.

If any senior leader expects you to lay out specific security objectives before you understand the needs of the organization, be on guard. The manner in which you develop relationships from the executive suite to the manufacturing floor helps in your openness to say: "I don't know" or "That is something I had not understood until just now." This will make you stand out from other newbies who came into their business with a bucket of instant answers.

Appearances to the contrary, if too-quick solutions are offered or presented, are likely to create fairly immediate pushback. It is true that in a small- or medium-sized facility, a security audit can be done and some appropriate changes made in half a day or less if that's how you want to do it. However, if you are in and out you are skipping over a wonderful learning opportunity with both the people and the culture of that facility. If you are too quick you may lose the opportunity to listen and learn about them and to get local employees involved in designing their own security plan.

Even more to the point, you lose an opportunity to build rapport and confidence between the security team and the employees and managers at a local facility. Ultimately, it is the people-intensive efforts that provide realistic flexibility and make any security plan work.

The security guidance and time you invest locally will eventually save a great deal of time, because a realistic security plan is locally sustainable. If the security plan is designed by those who manage and work at the facility, employees understand it and comply with it. In this way security becomes organically incorporated into the most essential and simple aspects of the business. When security planning is approached in this way you will find, in later years, that the security plans are appropriately reviewed, meaningfully updated, and creatively exercised as a matter of routine every year.

In the past, many organizations have experienced just the opposite. Security plans were imposed, simply an overlay of what someone, too frequently a consultant, thought or some "know it all" from headquarters would meet the needs of a given facility or operation. Many such plans were irrelevant to any specific security aspects or needs of the business or a particular facility. They were a cut and paste job, and usually rejected in practice by those who worked in or ran operations and told to make them "just fit."

Unfortunately, if a serious security incident occurs in an environment that lacks a realistic and well-integrated and responsive plan, no one knows how to respond. In some instances, the business or facility may become a crime scene. If this happens, some corporations never recover from these incidents, which could have been mitigated and managed better in the first place.

Real change is slow. For the security leader, it takes flexible leadership, values solid to the core, hard work, and a willingness to take risks. You will use every skill you have ever learned; to be successful you must be willing to learn new ones, both formally and informally, in a constant way.

Lifelong learning is absolutely essential; it includes equal parts of confidence and humility. These ingredients can transform your efforts, the work of your team, and will inevitably impact the quality of a security program. As you learn, you have the opportunity to move beyond security expertise to security know-how. It is the latter that catapults a business's security program from good to excellent and excellent to great.

Whatever your time estimate for building an integrated security program across a large enterprise, I suggest that you double or triple it. Implementing a security strategy in this way—one that is woven around and through the unique profit drivers of a business—will involve struggling with many obstacles, some of them unforeseen. You must persevere on the trail as you identify obstructions moving across the terrain of the business. Remember, although it is appropriate and to your advantage to seek some simple quick wins, what you are really looking for are sustainable long-term security results that help the business.

Establishing security is all about trust. Both you and the corporate leadership must allow the time to create trust from the very outset of any effort to develop a security plan.

5.6 LESSON #6: STAY IN TOUCH WITH YOUR PEERS

Who will be your sounding board when you are expected to have instant answers to long-standing security and organizational issues? What will you do, and whom will you call, when challenges become overwhelming?

There are many professional colleagues who truly understand what you are up against. They have already walked this trail. Be willing to cast ego issues aside and reach out to those who have been there before you. They will hear you when you are dealing with business leaders who think they know "all about security." They will know what it means to deal with the stress of early breakfast meetings, late dinner meetings, and time after that catching up with e-mail.

Claiming the support of colleagues at the same level, especially if they have security expertise and know-how in the same industry, can be a lifesaver. Discussing what you are experiencing can also give you greater perspective and objectivity, as can keeping a journal, not just on what is happening, but on how you feel about it. Nothing lightens a backpack like an occasional look at its contents and their weight. This is just common sense.

Where do you find quality support? Probably the most widely known security organization is ASIS International (www.asisonline.org). Then there are organizations with special membership criteria for security leaders such as ISMA (www.isma.com) and the SEC (www.securityexecutivecouncil.com). There are also associations for a broad spectrum of industries, from airlines to food processing to utilities and export/import firms. Other groups are issue oriented, such as the ACFE (www.acfe.com) and the like.

Both ASIS and ACFE are excellent associations to start with; they each have local chapters as well as national programs. Their professional security training and certifications are excellent and internationally recognized.

There are also specialized organizations like CSI for information protection professionals. Almost every discipline in the field of security has an association worth exploring. For example, there are organizations that have strong ties with state and federal regulatory agencies or universities.

All these groups offer valuable information focused on specific security issues. Many organizations will want you and your membership dollars. It is wise to focus on those that are closest to your business, and to match the challenges you face with the focus of the organization.

Before you commit to a professional organization, ask around. Look for local mentors who have successfully transitioned from one line of work to another—especially if their history corresponds some-what with your own. Once you join an association, get to know the local chapter members and make yourself available to work with them on a security project of theirs, sharing with them your expertise. Such colleagues will provide you with a seasoned perspective on a myriad of security issues. These shared activities can build understanding and relationships that last decades.

I have found a unique level of professional sharing across the board in business security. Sometimes when you are facing a specific challenge, a friend will share a program that took years to build. The networks referred to here do not usually develop from sitting in free security seminars, from a webcast, or a vendor magazine. They are built on the mutual trust, the same way you build any solid relationship. There is nothing more essential to your success than having an extensive network of experienced friends whom you can call on at a moment's notice. To such a network, I owe some of my best experiences as a security leader.

5.7 LESSON #7: MAINTAIN YOUR SENSE OF HUMOR

If you are tagged as "the new Marshall in town," you might as well enjoy the humor. You may need to change some perceptions down the line, but you don't need to be solemn about it. Whatever your brand of humor, nourish it. A good laugh can defuse many a tense situation.

5.8 LESSON #8: PERFECT YOUR SUPPORT SKILLS

Most business leaders in large organizations expect to be able to turn to a trusted insider to address a wide spectrum of risks to the business. When there is a serious issue, *you* should be the one that management at all levels will turn to. In some instances, a perceived crisis may be traced to a poor choice of language, or confused communications in the business or even to incomplete or incorrect information.

At other times, you will be dealing with extremely sensitive and serious issues or incidents. Your management team will look to you for direction, next steps, and interventions. Other executives are unlikely to have a level of experience close to yours if a serious incident occurs, especially if you have had combat experience or held law enforcement positions.

It is possible for you to be called on to take responsibility in handling issues that affect employees, even though they are not directly workplace related. In the real world, there is a fine line between the public and personal needs of employees. For example, in one company, the family member of an employee was missing over a weekend. The employee was contacted by police, their family member's car had been found along the side of an interstate highway. There was no sign of foul play and no one was found.

Management requested that I reach out to the employee. The employee asked that we reach out to our law enforcement contacts and requested that our security team join actively in the search to help find the family member. A day later, the family member was found dead. At that point there was an agreement that because I knew the employee very well I was the best person to share this tough news.

Having been a marine burial officer, the one who hands the flag to the next of kin, I knew that I could do this notification in a caring and personal way. When the moment came to share the loss, though it was difficult, I was able to communicate with sensitivity, tenderness, and respect.

The business team at this company, from chairman to contract employees, never forgot how the security team helped deal with this tough incident. Such incidents illustrate a unique set of skills to help engage and communicate with others. In so doing it demonstrates abilities many, including ourselves, may never have envisioned as part of the job. At times we all need special support. In this case, helping to handle a very difficult non-job-related incident was not only a decent thing to do but also completely consistent with a core value of the organization: treat others the way we want to be treated.

5.9 LESSON #9: EXCEED EXPECTATIONS

When you are given access to the various departments of the business, it is important to communicate that you are there to drive business results. When you do this, people begin calling you because they recognize you have something to contribute to their success. When the phone rings, or the e-mail comes asking you to contact someone, you never know the scope of the issues. While most are minor, some may be major, and you don't have time to sort them out until you know what they are. It is critical that you respond. Failing to do so within 24 hours, at the most, will kill your reputation faster than anything else.

The other side of staying current and following up on requests is that folks will expect almost 24-hour service. When you begin supporting a 27,000-person global enterprise by yourself, without an excellent team in place, you have a very difficult, though not impossible, task. This is a quick way to learn the organization, where the security issues are, and which managers are cooperative. You must exceed their expectations in terms of response time and quality. This results in the security team quickly earning trust across the organization.

5.10 LESSON #10: BE AWARE OF SLIPPERY SLOPES

Companies today face major losses because of lack of accountability. It can be shocking to observe the lack of control over even their most valuable assets. Whatever happened to the clean desk policy, to segregation of duties, to keeping things locked up?

A major distribution company had a policy that at the end of the workday their drivers would drop trailers at the loading docks, and park tractors in a well-fenced and lighted area of the facility. One Monday morning we received a call that one of the tractors had been stolen. The chain securing gates to the facility's fence had been cut. This was a new tractor valued at over $200,000. The police had taken the report and put out detailed information on the rig.

When I asked who had access to the keys of the tractor, there was a very long pause. Finally, the caller said that the facility's "policy" was to leave the tractors unlocked, with the keys in the ignition. Initially, I thought this was a joke. Apparently, the practice started because employees would forget keys at home. Needless to say, a new policy went into effect immediately. Fortunately, the tractor was found 2 days later in good condition, in an alley a few miles away.

In addition to instances of carelessness, the ability of employees to appropriate, steal, or otherwise adversely impact a company's assets has grown with the capabilities of technology. As technology has gotten faster and smaller, it is evermore difficult to address these problems.

Some security professionals view issues such as this as an organizational slippery slope. If employees have access to open office supply rooms, or ignore it when business assets are taken for personal use, is the organization not establishing an environment that tacitly condones such practices? In an era when there is a distinct trend toward lessening meaningful controls, the security leader should, at the very least, be involved in the review of these and similar business controls. Many times this can result in saving the company significant financial resources.

5.11 LESSON #11: CHOOSE TO SPRINT!

Once you have a good sense of the business, consider some questions that will surface immediate opportunities for action.

- What opportunities can be identified to enhance safety and security simply by improving channels of communication or tweaking other small adjustments to internal business processes?
- What areas of risk/exposure can be mitigated at minimal expense?
- What three or four security issues must the business avoid? What assets or changes are needed to do so?
- What realignments of responsibility and accountability will both enhance security and help the business?

Be aware that with the last of these areas you may be stepping on some toes, unless managers are comfortable with what you are doing. You may actually lose valuable time and respect by taking on realignments for which the culture is not prepared.

Work first with those who want to work with you and deal first with areas focused on the first three questions. Producing meaningful results that helps to drive the business builds rapport, support, and momentum with internal business partners better than anything else. In helping them, your success becomes their success.

Most employees simply want to do their work and feel safe. They expect management to follow the same rules they do. One of the key behaviors for a safe workplace is being able to report offensive or troubling events and issues in a way that does not come back to haunt the person who makes the report. Establish a confidential reporting mechanism. This is one of the most important initiatives a company can take.

Perhaps reports are made through a 1-800 hotline, a company ethics program, or to a corporate security leader. Whatever method is used, it is crucial that the reported information must avoid being tracked back to a specific source or individual. There is only one exception to this rule, and that is when the information reported is not true and accurate. Short of false reporting, every incident needs to be taken seriously and appropriately reviewed, and with a final decision it is important to also communicate timely to whoever provided the information.

As success begins with employees, there are some simple and proven initiatives that are cost-effective. These are good starting points early on in your employment.

- Initiate a security section on the company's intranet home page and include helpful security hints for home, school, shopping, and other activities away from the worksite.
- Indicate how to share confidential security information with corporate security through e-mail, voicemail, or other methods.
- Provide a 24/7 toll-free phone number for situations involving threats or bodily harm; set up a quick and effective response to such reports.
- Place posters in common areas providing the kinds of information listed above.
- Establish training programs on a variety of security issues. Make these part of company orientation for those newly hired; make them available as in-service training programs to long-standing employees.
- Establish security awareness reviews for all levels of management up to and including all senior and executive leaders.

A key to success is to personally involve in designing and to participate in as many of these activities as possible. It keeps you close to employees and gives you a realistic sense of what is working and what is not. When a policy or procedure does not produce the right business results, get rid of it quickly. Don't let the cost of something keep it from the trash. Your task is to enhance the safety and security of employees and the business to not hang on to stuff. Just as other elements across the enterprise occasionally miss the mark, so will you. Get over it. Move on to handling issues with positive impact.

5.12 LESSON #12: EXPLORE COMMUNICATION PATHWAYS

Being able to communicate clearly and respectfully with others is a challenge, not just for a career, but also for life. We use eye contact, body language, and slang in ways that can be interpreted, and misinterpreted, in many ways, depending on the receiver's culture, history, and status. Building clear communication around a company's security issues requires patient exploration. Here is a good guideline: "If I care about you, I will speak so that you can listen. If you care about me, you will listen so that you can hear."

For example, I have noticed that IT enterprise teams have distinctly different understanding of the term "business continuity" than do operational leaders. This leads to understandable confusion, for example, when folks walk out of a meeting asking "What was that all about?" A good way to build a more precise understanding is to preface a discussion by asking three or four attendees questions such as: "When you hear someone use the term 'business continuity', what does that term mean to you?"

Alternatively, you may use PowerPoint slides to define terms or use a handout as an addendum. In any case, it is important that the terms you use deliver the meaning you intend.

Offering meaningful information supports business goals. You will hear attendees say: "This was time well spent; it helps me understand what this means to my operations. Thanks!" Establishing clarity at the beginning of every interaction, phone call, or meeting enhances positive outcomes for everyone. Failure to do so may leave people shrugging their shoulders and feeling they have wasted their time.

Your choice of words also sets a tone. Seldom has the word "crisis" ever crossed my lips in a corporate setting. As a security leader, you are there to be the coolest head in the room. Every word counts. When you are dealing with a workplace violence incident, the raising of the national alert level, a plunge in company's value in the stock market, ethical accusations against leaders, or similar threats, you may be asked to meet with the CEO or leadership council, and to assist them in facing the threat.

Most security leaders agree that the sooner the organization engages you, the better. At times, if you have the appropriate law enforcement relationships, you may be the conduit to bring distressing news from the public sector to the attention of company leaders. Be prepared to be among the calmest voices in the room.

Research on crisis management shows:

- At least 60% of initial reports are factually incorrect.
- Crisis reporting, especially by the media, is dramatic, dynamic, and unfocused. It is often confusing.
- The desire to know the specifics before they are available can trip up even the most experienced security professionals.

Your task is to work through every aspect of the situation. This is one of the times you can become truly invaluable to your business. I call it executive hand-holding.

You can prepare for such incidents by gradually and tactfully educating C-level executives about what real security entails. Ordinarily, their professional development may only have prepared them to ask cursory questions at budget time, such as: "What does the business get with these IT security costs?" After hundreds of extensive conversations with board of directors and senior corporate leaders at all levels, I realized that none of them had spent time in learning the fundamental principles of security operations. This will likely be true for you too.

Traditionally, they never had a college- or graduate-level course in business concepts for security, managing incidents of fraud, or dealing with workplace violence. When possible take every legitimate opportunity to give them a little orientation before serious threats occur.

Clarity and collaboration regarding security must be based on solid information. To develop an effective security program, you must go after information the same way as corporate audit, business development, and operations managers do. The security information you want to target has to do with actual inventory balances (not merely shrinkage), employee and management productivity issues (not merely workplace violence), and successful hiring practices (not merely background checks).

This means that you tailor a meaningful security message for the business when the timing is right. You can only do this once you know what is going on. Of course, you will ensure that background investigations are adequate; you will try to reduce threats to work environments; you will deal with theft issues.

Once you understand the needs of the organization, you will craft a 30-second vision summary of what you do and how you do it. If you do this too quickly, you will have to revise it repeatedly; changing messages are confusing to everyone. At one company, it was well over a year when the vision summary for corporate security was expressed as: corporate security focuses on the safe, secure delivery of our products to customers.

That one sentence captured what our security team was about: we strategized to protect our employees as our internal customers; to ensure the integrity of employee and customer information; to engage electronic system security issues related to computers, phone, radio, video, and alarms to safeguard our facilities; to look after our corporate brand. The vision summary only came from a firm understanding of the business as well as our role in it.

In most instances, a vision summary should encapsulate the scope of your authority and responsibility and create a basis for appropriate decision making.

Realistic collaboration is at the core of good communication. Today's executives know that strong internal collaboration is a force multiplier that delivers business results. To be truly effective, collaboration emanates from an individual to a team, and beyond to an extended team (all employees) and eventually becomes integral to the business culture. It continually fosters creative solutions for the business. Whether in sunshine or storm, clear communication is at the heart of every effort to collaborate.

Challenges

It is only by solidly learning the day-to-day business operations that you can prepare to handle crises well. Bringing a balanced and disciplined approach to address individual and organizational fear is tough stuff. Dealing with stalking incidents, major frauds, embezzlements, shootings involving death, and national crises involves tapping into a wide variety of skills. When faced with such circumstances, you may be stressed and tested as never before. One thing is certain: how you communicate, how you manage, how you react, and how you render support sends a lasting impression to everyone in the business.

Although I have often found such situations to be among my greatest challenges, one of my natural strengths is having a high level of empathy. This enables me to balance issues for both criminal and victim depending on who we may be dealing with in a given situation. This ability has served me well, both in public law enforcement and private corporate security roles. Each of us comes with gifts and liabilities. Develop your gifts and supplement for your liabilities by continuously learning and reaching out to your peers; building a team that works can make it all come together successfully.

In communicating with others when dealing with serious issues or incidents in the business, strive for accuracy, not drama. Strive for empathy, not condemnation. Strive for clear communication, not complexity. These habits will stand you in good stead when you are faced with an unexpected incident.

6.1 THE FIRST INCIDENT

As a security leader with just several months on the job in a major corporation, I faced one such scenario. Fortunately, I had informed senior leaders that if they noticed anything out of the ordinary in their business operations, or just something that made them uncomfortable, I was only a phone call away and happy to help them figure out what was going on.

Uncovering one of the largest embezzlements in the history of the company began when I received a simple phone call. Recently, the company's treasury office had been receiving requests for manual checks to be cut for a number of small IT vendors. The invoices had been properly authorized and signed, but were being personally hand delivered by a senior manager to the company treasury. This person had the reputation of being very controlling, arrogant, and demanding. He indicated that the invoices were from small specialty vendors needed to be paid immediately—in fact, he would like to hand deliver the checks himself.

However, the treasury office was on a very tight schedule with a very high-priority assignment involving the entire department. The decision was made that requests for manual checks would be denied. When this senior manager showed up at the company's treasury department, he threw a fit. As a result his request was fulfilled, but as it turns out for the last time. Because he was especially belligerent about the new policy, it raised the hackles of a few employees who were upset by his arrogance, and they called security. Something just did not seem right and this senior manager seemed very nervous. I asked them to run a simple computer review of the vendor accounts and to provide me with a copy of any further information they felt was important and left it at that.

The documents arrived and after reviewing them within a few days, we determined that the vendors were phony. We also determined that the work which was being billed was actually being done by another segment of our global company. In less than a week, we discovered that over seven hundred thousand dollars had been embezzled in less than 18 months.

This was our second significant embezzlement within a year and a half. The case came to light because I made it a point get to know the employees in the treasury operation and had had some conversations regarding what we were doing and the purposes of the security team.

The process this employee was using was simple and fairly well hidden; until we took a hard look at facts. As we pulled apart how this was happening, we were able to restrict information about the case to five employees. Subsequently, this senior employee was convicted. Not only was there a no trial guilty plea, but total restitution was also made; the individual was sentenced and served time.

6.2 HANDLING SURPRISES

It was a prior case of fraud in the same corporation that put me on the road to recovering big profits for the business. Success often depends on the willingness of others to make security aware of such an opportunity.

An advantage of having a background in law enforcement is that you know how to deal with surprises. The HR vice president came to my office to say a 23-year employee, well known and trusted throughout the business, had been identified for manipulating accounts under her control. I offered to interview the employee but did not know the particulars of the case. As I was leaving my office, I grabbed a large expandable file as a prop to my conversation with her. I told her that we knew what was going on regarding certain funds that she had diverted and suggested that she tell me about it. Although we knew that there were thousands of dollars missing, no one really knew the extent of the fraud. At that time, the best information we had was that perhaps twenty thousand dollars may be involved.

At the end of the interview, the employee admitted that she had embezzled very large amounts of money over the previous 3 years. She described the techniques she used and was permitted to leave after the interview. I asked that if she recalled additional information that would be helpful in clearing up this matter, to please call my cell phone. By the end of that day, the employee had called me three more times giving me additional details about the techniques she used to embezzle these funds. In the end, we determined that she had embezzled more than two hundred thousand dollars, over a period of just a few years.

This very first corporate security investigation in the history of the company led to collaboration among HR, security, finance, and senior management, as well as to recovering major portions of these losses and returned them to net earnings. The confidential manner in which security managed this problem quickly opened doors to other senior business leaders who were then open to discuss security concerns and issues in their operations.

It took a number of discussions with the senior management team as we moved the case forward to the district attorney for prosecution. From the outset of my employment, we had an agreement with executives that sound criminal cases we unearthed would be handed over to law enforcement and that when this happened, we were no longer in control of outcomes. This level of clarity is critical.

Finally, with the encouragement of executive management, this case was turned over for prosecution. As it went through the criminal justice system, I routinely briefed these business leaders every 10 days or so. However, do not presuppose that security's job is mostly about tracking down theft.

6.3 ASSAULTIVE BEHAVIOR IN THE WORKPLACE

Surveys show that the primary security problem in America's work environment is assaultive behavior in the workplace. National statistics reflect this trend. When it comes to saving lives, there is a simple rule: any threat to persons needs to become priority one. Everything else goes on the back burner until the threat allegations are resolved or removed.

In the following instance, we were just plain lucky that no loss of life occurred. I was traveling and a member of my security team received a phone call from a field manager on a Saturday at 7:00 a.m. The manager had been contacted by a federal law enforcement agency asking if a person named Dutch was one of his employees. Apparently, Dutch had made over a dozen calls threatening the lives of various company managers, by name. Dutch indicated he already etched the names of three supervisors on bullets. The law enforcement agency wanted to advise us of this situation and suggested that the company take some action.

Dutch was an employee of the company for 4 years. Dutch's background check had surfaced several "do not hire" indicators; however, he had skills that were in high demand for the business unit and so it was decided to go ahead and hire him. It was a local management decision despite this past employment history. Within a year, Dutch was being investigated by company's HR department for making threats. Most of the employees who worked in the same facility were afraid of Dutch and some were terrified.

Dutch was a huge man and his size was as intimidating as his actions. Divorced, with no close relationships, it was common knowledge that he had threatened to kill his estranged family members, saying, for example, that he should have killed his ex-wife and children so that he would not have to pay child support. As we began looking into this over the next 24 hours, it appeared that the only consistent social contact in Dutch's life was his work.

Dutch was also described as a survivalist. He had told others he was prepared for anticipated disruptions, political or otherwise, by stockpiling food and water, taking emergency medical training, preparing for self-defense and self-sufficiency, building structures that would help him to disappear, such as having hidden underground shelters. Finally, Dutch was a loner who boasted of owning a variety of weapons.

Discussions with local managers and others revealed that 2 years earlier there had been a workplace shooting close to, but unrelated to, our facility just down the street. That day, Dutch was out in the field. When our employees heard the news, most of them assumed that Dutch had been the shooter. One said: "We thought that Dutch had finally lost it."

Members of the security team knew we needed to carefully think through our options and that we needed the agreement of top executives for whatever plan we adopted. We had to buy some time to consult with local law enforcement and to develop a protection strategy for the facility. By late Saturday afternoon, our initial plan was in place. We would place Dutch on administrative leave with pay. HR, senior field managers, and local managers were in agreement with our initial plan to buy time and that it was a good first step. We ended the phone call thinking we had bought some time; however, our plan never had a chance to work.

Monday morning came fast. Very early, I was on my way to the office when my cell phone rang. A member of the security team had just gotten off the phone and was told Dutch was already in the field and not on administrative leave contrary to our agreed upon plan. It turned out that overnight there was an urgent repair that had to happen. Two local managers made the decision that Dutch should make the repair, despite our previous conversations and with no further discussion with corporate security.

We all knew that the federal law enforcement agency had warned that if Dutch makes one more threatening phone call, we will have him arrested. By the time I had gotten to the office, Dutch had already made another such call and was arrested for making threats to kill using an interstate telecommunications device, that is, a cell phone. Dutch was already in custody. Having law enforcement engaged on the federal and local levels really restricted our options. We had no idea how long Dutch would remain in custody. Everything was a mess and we needed more information.

The local manager's unilateral decision to send Dutch out to handle a repair had placed the business in a very tenuous position and its employees in serious danger. Fortunately for us, the federal law enforcement agency had a solid case. After Dutch was arrested, our security team worked closely with local law enforcement, the FBI, and the USSS. Search warrants were obtained; firearms were confiscated. Dutch was arraigned in federal court and remanded to the custody of the US Marshal until initial court hearings could be started.

Some employees continued to express concern; others were downright fearful that Dutch would direct his anger back at his former coworkers—that he would make bail and be back on the street. This fear continued for several months, as Dutch awaited sentencing. Over the course of several months, we worked with over a 100 employees, and in some cases families, to address individual and collective fears. It was a very long process.

In the end, everyone was safe. Dutch was convicted. He subsequently was relocated to a facility several hundreds of miles away and in another state. Considerable learning had taken place along the way. I doubt that anyone involved in this incident will ever forget it.

The business had skated on thin—very thin—ice.

Not every workplace violence occurrence has a successful ending. When a company has international operations, it is important to communicate clearly, with very specific directives, so that nothing is misunderstood. However, sometimes even the most detailed instructions reinforced by management are ignored.

Company Three was building a new facility in another country, to replace one that had been totally destroyed; the company had decided, as the new facility was being built, to retain our workforce of over a 1,000 employees and to continue to pay them. After several months, the new plant being built would soon go into production, even though many of the business control systems, such as payroll, were incomplete. In normal business operations, all employees received their pay via on-site ATM currency machines.

Our manufacturing division informed us that ATM installations were going to be delayed and that they were going to pay employees in cash. In advance of this taking place, we decided to send a corporate security team to the new facility to assess what additional security measures should be followed to protect employees and payroll during paydays.

Our team reviewed every facet of procedures from the time the cash was delivered via armored truck to the actual payment of employees; we made specific recommendations and briefed on-site management. Because there were other communication issues with this facility's senior management team, the security team met with them and presented our recommendations. They agreed our security instructions would be followed and implemented before the next payroll arrived.

Ten days later, payroll worth several hundred thousand dollars arrived, delivered by armored car, and taken into the facility. Shortly after, a hold-up occurred and the entire payroll was stolen. As the robbers were departing, a manufacturing employee who had been on break, not realizing what was happening, approached the robbers. He was shot and killed.

These events traumatized this entire manufacturing workforce. Neither the local nor senior management teams had implemented any of the recommendations corporate security had recommended. These events occurred on foreign soil in a country that has less than a 5% conviction rate for major felonies. We engaged a well-recognized private investigations firm to work with law enforcement and prosecutors at several levels, eventually all five robbers were arrested and convicted. It took nearly 5 years.

The bad news was that we lost an employee. From my days of combat in Vietnam, through our years in DEA field operations with agents and other law enforcement officers dealing with all kinds of violence, this was the only incident where someone was killed. I feel it to this day.

6.4 THREATS TO CORPORATE ASSETS

Occasionally, you will uncover threats to the business that, while not directly related to what people usually think of as "security," are a potential source of major property loss or worse. It was by listening carefully to an operational manager that I discovered threats to some microwave systems located in towers that controlled both the production of the business and also balanced and protected millions of dollars' worth of core business assets.

For about 10 years, the financial and maintenance responsibility for these towers had been transferred from a core unit of the business to IT. The IT department had fought for jurisdiction of the microwave systems and included them in its communications budget. IT executives convinced senior leaders that this move would save resources and create economies of scale.

When the towers were transferred to IT, they had been very carefully maintained and were in excellent condition because those in charge of operations understood the importance of tower maintenance for the protection of their core business assets. Unfortunately, this concept was lost on IT management. Over time, the microwave and tower maintenance was indistinguishable in the IT budget. As budget cuts were imposed, tower maintenance was not only cut back but it was also eliminated. Business operations managers who relied on the microwave tower systems were unaware of this change.

When joining this company, part of my task was to build a security program that was aligned with the needs of business operations. The above situation came to light one day as I was learning about some of the company's critical infrastructure and how important these microwave systems were to one of our core business units. Almost as a side comment, one manager said there was a real vulnerability. He indicated that even after repeated warnings to the IT budget management team, "no one was willing to take it on." As I pursued the conversation, the manager indicated that the towers of the system had not been maintained for several years and they were in such a bad shape that some could partially fail and others might collapse.

This one manager and a few of his employees had repeatedly warned about the consequences of this lack of routine maintenance—all to no avail. At this point, several towers needed significant overhaul. As a result of us bringing this to the attention of senior operations and executive leaders including the chief information officer (CIO), the budgets for tower and microwave maintenance were immediately realigned back to operations. A major fiasco had been avoided.

One of the things we learned from this incident was to listen to company personnel who know contract management. Any security contract that is managed outside your core security team needs to be audited carefully, especially if you are to take responsibility for its oversight. It is very easy to be misled, unless you or a knowledgeable member of your team has a sound understanding of security contract management. Once again, this is an example of people working in the day-to-day operations of a company who deserve to be heard. They will often note real trouble spots that may be overlooked by others.

6.5 DEALING WITH PROBLEM PERSONNEL

Sometimes, business risks present themselves in the person of certain employees. In one company I worked for, shortly after my arrival as security leader, an employee from another corporate function came and introduced himself. Let's call him Picasso. He seemed eager to talk and I was more than willing to listen. Picasso told me he was the corporate emergency planner; he was also responsible for the company's extensive art collection. This seemed to me an odd mix of responsibilities. Picasso agreed and it seemed to me that he talked more about being the art docent than about emergency planning.

He was very up front about one thing; he did not like working where he was currently assigned. He said he was coming to me because he felt his emergency planning role was more aligned with the new security department. He was very well prepared and arrived with his resume in hand and asked that I review it. I agreed to do this, especially because one of my new responsibilities was to develop a company-wide emergency plan. By all indications, Picasso seemed full of energy and commitment. However, he liked neither his current nor his previous supervisor, both of whom were women.

Fast forward a few weeks. I was meeting with my boss and in almost a side comment he mentioned that the chairman thought it would be a good idea if Picasso, the emergency planner, was reassigned to my department. When I asked how the chairman knew this employee, I was told, "Because he has been in charge of corporate art for some years and in this capacity Picasso works with the chairman's wife who takes an active interest in art." I said I would like some time to consider this request and we agreed to again discuss it in a week or so. Although I had a few misgivings about the new arrangement, I accepted Picasso. That was mistake number one.

This new employee was eager to discover my thoughts on all kinds of security issues; he became overly helpful. When I was away on a trip to explore the company's operations, he arranged to have some very nice artwork placed in my office. After a few months, I was able to recruit an administrative assistant from within the company and was about to hire a new professional onto the security team to manage technical security issues. Because the new professional would be managing technical security systems across the organization and bringing parity to the emergency planner, I lobbied to get Picasso his first promotion in several years. Further, in order to update his skills, we arranged to have him attend a first-class business continuity seminar in New York City. Meanwhile, I continued to focus on learning business operations.

As I traveled, the new security team was dealing with a wide variety of tactical pop-up issues. I continued to get strange reactions from senior operational leaders in the field about Picasso—"oh, you mean the art enthusiast!" I explained that he was a good writer who knew both the organization and emergency planning as well as having responsibility for the corporate art collection.

Before long, Picasso became increasingly unhappy again, but this time it was with me. He was busily seeking to move higher in the organization, and his activities and demeanor were increasingly negative to the point of distraction. I did not have time to play his various games. He had politicked hard to move under the control of the COO. In short order, I supported his reassignment to the COO. Picasso was delighted; however, his karma was bad. His happiness was short-lived because his mentor, the COO, left the corporation unexpectedly and he was reassigned to the real estate operations. Picasso had gone full circle and was now in middle management in less than a year. Through my interactions with Picasso, I realized that even when people are treated fairly they are often about getting their own way. Picasso's personal insecurity just carried over to everything he did. I had learned a valuable lesson, but I was learning by making mistakes and had temporarily lost focus on the priority needs of the organization because of distractions like this.

6.6 HOW CHANGES IN CORPORATE STRUCTURE CAN AFFECT SECURITY

Sometimes, the security leader's position may be compromised by a series of complex corporate situations that arise from mergers and acquisitions.

I was on the senior management team of a company for 3 years when it was acquired. Before the acquisition, the new parent company called it a merger, but it definitely didn't turn out that way. During our 3 years as a stand-alone company, I reported to my company's HR senior vice president. He was not only an outstanding leader for HR but also largely responsible for enabling security to build solid relationships with all the members of the executive team and especially with the CEO and president. As a result, we had earned their support and trust, and they gave us a high degree of independence. Now our work of the previous 3 years was about to change.

After our company was acquired, we learned the parent company had just restructured their security function and a few months earlier hired a new security leader from a federal law enforcement agency. Following the merger, there were a series of HR meetings. Our HR management team was very open while our counterparts of the parent company were just the opposite. They preferred to take notes during our meetings and say little. From the very first meeting, it was evident that our new parent company intended to rely heavily on a security consulting firm they had used for the past few years.

Based on our discussions and glowing recommendations about this consulting firm's achievements, I was looking forward to learning more. I was unfamiliar with this firm, so I contacted a security colleague who was located in their city. I was very glad I made the call.

My friend used some choice language about the outfit. The first time I called him he said "Don't you know this outfit has been indicted? The state's attorney has charged them on multiple felony counts, including wiretapping." I sat in disbelief and took notes for the next hour, listening to a detailed account of the issues involved in the indictment and the reputation of the security firm. All that was alleged in the indictment involved firms other than our parent company, but the accusations were extremely sobering. The allegations needed exploration.

By the end of this conversation, I knew I needed to brief my senior management team and do some research with our general counsel. This was approved; our counsel contacted a law firm in the metropolitan area where the lawsuit had been filed and ordered up a copy of the indictment. It was in our office the next day. The indictment had confirmed our concerns. We decided not to disclose any of these issues when we first met with the owner of this consulting company. My executives gave me the latitude to raise the issue internally, as I saw fit. We wanted to see if any of the information about the indictment would be voluntarily shared.

The new parent company's head of HR was a woman whom I shall call Dorothy. Dorothy requested we travel to our soon-to-be new headquarters for a security meeting. She was intent on meeting at her headquarters and to introduce the owner from this security consulting firm. The entire direction of the meeting was focused on the consulting firm's wonderful skills, capabilities, and results. The firm's owner played back all that Dorothy was saying. It was clear that both she and the consultant were going to be making all the security decisions.

Also present was the new parent company's vice president for security. He appeared to be tense and was silent throughout the meeting. I found this odd. I had consulted a few colleagues about him; he had excellent credentials and a stellar reputation. He had transitioned recently from a major law enforcement position, had been hired by the COO of parent company, but had been unaware that he would report directly to Dorothy.

It was clear to me that there was little possibility of an effective security relationship between our security team, Dorothy, and her consultant. As the meeting broke up, the vice president of security asked if I would like to visit one of their new facilities. On the way, we engaged in normal small talk and as we arrived I asked: what do you know about Dorothy's consultant? I sensed he did not have a clue about the indictment issue. He asked in return, what are you talking about?

I confidentially shared with him the information we had uncovered. He had left a very promising mid-level career in law enforcement; clearly, he was dazed. Within days, Dorothy was informed about the indictment, which she insisted was "trumped-up." Once that card was played, I sensed Dorothy was determined to get rid of or dissolve our security team any way she could.

However, it was also clear that, given a free hand, she could also be her own undoing. Dorothy's behaviors became increasingly extreme. After several months, she was gone. This is being shared not just for the story itself. What we had done to earn the trust of our senior and executive leaders over the preceding 3 years trumped every move Dorothy attempted. Our best protection in this situation was the level of uncompromising trust of our management team had in us as we went through this merger. What had been built over 3 years was not destroyed in 3 months. Our team was greatly relieved.

6.7 SECURITY PROBLEMS THAT ARISE OUT OF DISORGANIZATION

Then there was Ralph. Ralph had been a part-time reserve police officer prior to his joining a company where I became security leader. At the time of Ralph's arrival, the company was small, with operations in only one state. Corporate security had limited duties. Ralph's principal job was that of driving the chairman.

Fast forward several years. Through a series of reorganizations and poor management decisions, the company's first corporate security team was dissolved. Only Ralph hung on. He lasted in the company for over 20 years and was bounced from one staff to another. Ralph had never had the benefit of a good leader to work with him. According to him, he was always on call for the chairman and he knew he could play this card at will, which he often did. As a result, Ralph had no accountability except when his pager went off. Even the chairman's executive assistant at times had difficulty reaching him or knowing where he was. This went on for years.

Over time, Ralph's duties grew to include checking the chairman's home and property, watering house plants, responding to alarms, monitoring home contractors, and similar informal duties.

As a reserve police officer, Ralph could legally carry a concealed firearm. It was not uncommon for Ralph to walk around headquarters displaying a sidearm. Although this unnerved some employees, no one dared say anything. In the years prior to September 11, 2001, the company had grown considerably and now had operations in more than 15 states.

In one instance, after 9/11, Ralph arrived at corporate headquarters dressed in military camouflage and combat boots armed not only with a sidearm but also with a semiautomatic rifle. Needless to say, this made even the chairman nervous. In the aftermath of 9/11, the business reestablished corporate security. There were now a multitude of security issues that needed to be addressed and included a meaningful strategy and what to do with Ralph. When I was hired to be the security leader, the first person assigned to the security team was Ralph; but there was an issue—he was upset because he had not been considered for the senior security position.

Because Ralph had been with the company as a loyal employee for many years, we afforded him opportunities to learn new skills, though none of these opportunities resulted in any tangible benefit to the company. Finally, a decent arrangement was worked out and Ralph retired from the business.

His situation was one symptom of a much larger series of organizational issues, including the impact of the previous failure of the entire security function. The legacy of the previously dysfunctional security team and the considerable internal turmoil they created resulted in a lot of negative perceptions about what we would be about.

Such dynamics and situation present tremendous challenges to a new security leader. There was never any overt opposition across the business to the new security program primarily because we had come on board to deal with post-9/11 issues. However, because of the hidden history, it took considerably longer than expected for our efforts to take root and succeed.

It takes real leadership and quiet determination, as well as skill, compassion, and peer support, to deal with the Ralphs, Dorothys, and Picassos you may come across. In the presence of a "Dutch," it also took luck and a company's willingness to learn from its mistakes. The resolution of embezzlements and of the near-fiasco of the microwave towers took teamwork, careful listening, and the courage of several employees to confront corporate politics and inertia. To our sorrow, in one of our experiences, we learned from the death of an employee how important compliance to security directives and plans can be, especially in a cross-cultural environment.

As we travel these roads and confront these and other challenges, perhaps we learn more from human failure and vulnerability, than from our successes.

CHAPTER 7

Losses and Gains Along the Way

Something's lost and something's gained in living every day.
Judy Collins, *Both Sides Now*

It has been said that if you think education is expensive, try ignorance. If you think providing security is costly, try neglecting it. In this chapter, I will discuss the importance of:

- Earning their trust
- Valuing their time as well as their profits
- Communicating well across the business
- Comparing security expense to its value for the business
- Realizing and communicating the impact and cost of fraud and lost assets
- Effectively communicating these costs in business terms
- Communicating effectively with senior leaders in order to have a positive business impact
- Determining the real costs of any security program you inherit as well as the money required for the one you envision

When you begin your tasks as a new security leader, be prepared to take considerable time to determine the real costs of whatever security measures are already in place. Sometimes businesses are penny-wise and pound-foolish in this regard. For example, you may discover that there are costs for security related to its headquarters and other facilities, inventory, information, and employees; perhaps these costs have escalated automatically over time without anyone really considering the effectiveness of such outlays in protecting the business.

As you begin to explore, know that you may be treading on a rocky terrain. Sometimes operational managers are protective of the security and are unwilling to share its costs to their business unit. Perhaps they are unsure of its costs. Or perhaps they know what it costs, but don't have any notion of the precise return on their investment, or lack thereof. You must have the backing of your corporate leaders, especially those in the C-suite, in order to study and really get to the costs of security measures already in place.

The task of the security team is to foster positive business impact while keeping people and assets safe. Executives have the capacity to leverage the efforts of the security team as you identify and prioritize issues across the enterprise. If the organization is serious about dealing with security issues in an effective and timely manner, senior leaders must be available to you when you need to see them.

The following executives are key players in the security of any business. Depending on the configuration of an organization, others may also be very important. Strive to work closely with:

- The general counsel because of regulatory, compliance, and corporate governance. Other than reporting to the CEO, the general counsel is generally the ideal executive for the head of security to report to because of the overall scope of the position's responsibilities.
- The chief financial officer (CFO) because of audit and financial control issues, and the Sarbanes–Oxley and Graham–Rudman Act.
- The executive HR officer because of employee background information, workplace violence or intimidation issues, workman's compensation, time and attendance fraud, and similar issues.
- The COO because of the need to coordinate with senior operational leaders to resolve external and internal threats, thefts, and other sensitive issues.
- The CIO because of the need to integrate and manage ever-expanding information security issues across the enterprise.

There is a cautionary note here: how you manage access to executives sends a strong signal to them, either that you are providing substantive support to the organization, or that you are on an ego trip, or worse, that you are "crying wolf." If at any point they determine that you are out to make headlines for yourself, your reputation and credibility will suffer ever after. You must deliver an analysis of security issues that is brief, clearly focused on business outcomes with three or four options indicating likely the positives and negatives of each option.

There is a concept referred to as return on management or ROM. (See *Performance Measurement and Control Systems for Implementing*

Strategy by Robert Simons.) I first learned of ROM at an ISMA seminar for executive security leaders conducted by Dr. Simons of the Harvard Business School. Dr. Simons describes ROM as "the amount of productive organizational energy released divided by the amount of management time and energy invested." His focus is very direct. If you, as the senior security leader, intend to maintain the active support of key executives, never waste their time.

A quick and easy way to discover how to deliver high-quality ROM in the culture of an organization is to cultivate several internal mentors who directly report to senior executives. For example, find out how the CEO prefers to have information presented from various functions—such as finance, marketing, operations, and sales—and staff.

As crazy as this may sound, some executives only want to hear good news. Others will want all the news, and in very specific ways: verbal briefings, PowerPoint slides, written reports. Some like to receive information in private; others prefer to have their direct reports or team present. You must also offer executives a choice of options to consider regarding how to resolve the issues you present. It is essential that you first do your homework and know the most effective ways in which to approach them before contacting them to do a presentation. Contacting them before you are ready can set up a difficult situation if the executive says: "Hey, I have some time now; why don't you just come up and give me your presentation."

Over time, I have learned to listen actively and attentively for nuances that have helped me to communicate with executives. Active listening involves noting body language and tone of voice as well as choice of words and the intensity of overall communication. For example, I have noted that sometimes:

- Executives place a high priority on being financially and sometimes on being personally secure.
- For many, preparations for Y2K was the first instance when any of them had taken a broader view of security.
- When 9/11 came along with the resulting compliance and regulatory issues and how they continue to evolve have reinforced in business executives the importance of business continuity, risk management, and security across the business.
- Business leaders are often more vigilant with the businesses finances than they are astute about security.

- If they have served in the military, particularly if this was a positive experience for them, they may be more attuned to security issues and they may relate their military experience in terms of security.
- They may be aware of how other corporations handle security based on outside meetings they attend.
- Their grasp of security may be limited to asking cursory questions at budget time.
- Their image of security may be clouded by a personal incident, for example, the last time a cop pulled them over for some traffic violation or their impression of the last *CSI* episode they saw on TV.
- The value they place on security for the business parallels the support you may initially expect from them.

I encourage you to pay attention to such details and to use them well in framing contexts that will help you relate to a particular business leader's security concerns. Listen well and maintain impeccable confidentiality.

As issues surface and you handle them effectively across the breadth of the enterprise, you are delivering important results and convincing executives, one at a time, that you are on their team.

The quick rise of the security function from the guard shack to the front office still leads to misunderstandings; a mature business model for the security leader is still evolving. Therefore, one cannot assume that what security can contribute to a business is obvious to all involved.

My good friend Bill Dunne shared with me a case in point. Bill, a former senior Secret Service Agent, has made a successful transition from the public to the private sector. When he retired from federal service, he became the head of security for one of Chicago's financial exchanges. He shared with me that at an early meeting with the board of directors, he was asked to explain and justify his security budget.

About half way through his presentation, Bill stopped. He could see that he had lost his audience—that he needed to communicate differently in a way the board could relate to. He paused and simply said: "Look, you are all businessmen. You understand business risk much better than I. However, I understand security risks and how the lack of security can compromise an entire enterprise."

Bill continued: "Everything I have described up to this point is aimed at one goal: reducing risk for the exchange. As board members who deal with business risk, you know that when risk is reduced, shareholder value goes up. It's that simple. If I do my job right, security will mitigate a variety of risks that could otherwise spell disaster for the business. For example, insurance costs could go down."

The board chairman replied: "That, I understand!" As a result, Bill worked with the CFO and others to reduce business risk in all areas of the exchange. At the same time, this business focus heightened the effectiveness of several security initiatives, integrating them into many aspects of the exchange's operations.

Bill successfully translated security objectives into business terms; board members related to these. As a result, he developed a completely new relationship between business and security at the exchange. From that point forward, he had the complete support of the board of directors as well as the exchange's executive management team.

As you communicate with business leaders, your momentum builds with each step, although the process may be as exhausting as it is rewarding. You are likely to be putting in very long days at the beginning. However, building these relationships is foundational. It takes time, but this is time that will repay the business a hundredfold.

I recommend to you *The Effective Executive in Action*, by Peter F. Drucker, especially pages 70 and 74. Drucker underlines the importance of understanding your organization's culture, especially when you are blazing new trails. Take time to consider an approach that is tailored to the strengths of the executives to whom you are making a presentation.

> *Think through your own strengths and those of your bosses. Work out a plan of continuous learning whereby ... you do all you can to make the strengths of your bosses productive by reinforcing their strengths and by shielding them from the effects of their weaknesses .... Strong people (like executives) always have strong weaknesses too. Performance can only be built on strengths. What matters most is the ability to do the assignment.*
>
> **Drucker, ibid.**

On the other hand, if you mishandle the first issues you confront in any way, including the manner and timing of your communication with executives, you may be setting yourself up for a short and frustrating future. This is not only personally disappointing but also costly for the business; it sometimes also creates tremendous resistance to dealing effectively with security in the organization, because there are always those who are eager to say: "See, it doesn't work."

Such folks are always too busy to care about anything meaningful in security unless it directly affects them. They may listen respectfully, but security is not on their real agenda. Unfortunately, some of these executives may have broad organizational influence, for example, in determining hiring or budgets.

Discount this at your peril.

Security leaders acknowledge that industries that have a mature infrastructure, such as manufacturing, utilities, and distribution companies, pose special challenges. This is especially true when creative processes, open communication, and constant improvements are not part of the company's culture. Such environments tend to be highly resistant to change.

In these environments, it is common to discover some who manage in only one way: by making demands. Persons who exercise such a coercive management style succeed by keeping everything and everyone off balance. Sometimes they require minute reorganizing of information into an endless variety of formats; they may not allow you to make presentations until the timing is right, and they may insist that they alone may present material to other members of the executive management team.

Once there was an executive, I'll call Joanne, who was a ballerina in the dance of delay and diversion. She had a magnificent education, excellent credentials, and was very polished. However, I felt unusually uncomfortable in her presence. Then I noticed that if I proposed a line of action that seemed good for the security program, she would:

- Make a suggestion or two and indicate that the objectives needed to be more refined.
- Work me in between other meetings, which always ran over and our meeting would be routinely cut short, and indicate that the revised suggestions still "needed a little tweaking."

- Lay out further suggestions at a subsequent meeting and moved around meetings that invariably resulted in further delays.
- And finally, be much too busy with real priority business issues to see me again and one of the issues included a golf game.

The theme of this "dance of diversion" is to delay in order to control.

These tactics of derailing, stalling, and appearing to be indecisive have nothing to do with shaping the right business message for Joanne or the business. It had everything to do with wearing down subordinates. It may take considerable personal reflection, as well as consultation with outside and trusted security colleagues, to understand what is going on. Initially, you may feel only confusion, frustration, and at times anger. What you come to realize is that your program is stuck; it is not gaining traction in the business.

Although sometimes procrastination in the form of constant "modifications" may result from a superior's lack of personal confidence, occasionally it is a way of derailing, discrediting, or even destroying the effectiveness of the security program. Occasionally, you may find that this is a comfort zone for lawyers and general counsels. We are all aware of how defense attorneys routinely use delay techniques. It is always advisable to maintain detailed notes and backup documentation regarding delays to security initiatives, especially in this case. This is to ensure that when security issues are identified to management, they are dealt with in a timely manner.

In addition to documenting, decide that you will maintain your cool. As you walk through these minefields, take care to maintain your own personal balance. Tap into your support systems. Keep your focus on goals rather than difficult persons. Remember that executives themselves and the organization are works in progress. If you decide to tackle head-on the inappropriate tactics of a coworker or supervisor, be sure you are well prepared. It takes candor, clarity, and courage to do so, and it should only be done for the good of the organization.

Many times leaders can be won over simply by reinforcing the concept that you are there to make their jobs easier and to help them drive positive business results by placing your professional skills at their service and that of the corporation. That should be your only agenda.

Despite such frustrating situations, it is of paramount importance for today's businesses to have a steady security leader who has experience in dealing with serious incidents and issues; such a leader is invaluable to the business. Managing with security know-how brings to the corporate table an understanding and perspective regarding some emergencies that many business leaders have only seen on television. The dynamics of a high-pressure incident often change with the presence of a security leader who is knowledgeable and is providing sound judgment; the result is a better outcome for the organization and for all concerned.

Once you drill into and fully expose the existing security costs, you are in a position to determine how to save money without sacrificing security. This is a complex task, as security issues today involve every aspect of the business. The following list indicates risk areas you should consider:

Third-party management	Capacity	Criminal acts
Cultural shift	Data integrity	Dividend risk
Employee	Environmental	Events
Fraud	Health/safety	Industrial
IT	Litigation	Mergers/acquisitions
Operations	Outsourcing	Partnerships
Political	Product	Projects
Regulatory	Sabotage	Supply chain

Executives always want to save money without sacrificing quality in their operation. Look especially for some simple ways to minimize risks, some quick wins by changing or refining processes that yield better security practices and business outcomes.

Your next task is to compare the existing security expenses to the real security challenges facing the business. In your conversations, meetings, and visits as you get to know and understand the business, you will likely learn and surface security challenges and opportunities.

While you are doing this, it is often a great time to experience differing aspects of your business culture. Sometimes this can be just as important, if not more important, in understanding the business reasons why different challenges exist in the same corporation. For example, parts of the organization that were merged into your business, or acquired, may only have a partially integrated security function because of internal politics. I have experienced very-well-run parts of the business that didn't even know that a security team existed.

Some areas of the business may also have been permitted to continue systems that parallel other identical processes in the corporation. If such duplications and gaps stay hidden, or if leaders avoid dealing with them—this is not uncommon—you may eventually have to deal with a serious security event. Where gaps existed and were not discovered, I have seen situations where the security team was held responsible because they had failed to identify and resolve the gaps in security.

Once you understand the business and how such duplications and gaps may have been perpetuated, you are in a position to propose a meaningful security program that is integrated into every aspect of the business. This can be demonstrably cost-effective, and it will potentially save the company millions of bottom-line that were lost or otherwise wasted.

Another word of caution here: the manner in which you address such issues is critically important. In public service, much of my professional experience was based on taking charge and initiating actions, which I saw to be necessary to achieve law enforcement goals. I had adequate, if not ideal, personnel to immediately direct toward resolving a particular dilemma and a clear chain of command on which to rely. In other words, the culture was with me. If necessary, I could be confrontational in pushing a specific agenda.

This approach does not work in corporate America. When I began working in business security, we were at the end of the organization's budget line. In order to achieve necessary business goals, I struggled to discover an alternative to direct confrontation. Feeling like "an army of one," I had to learn to shape my own behaviors to achieve the best possible results. This was a huge challenge.

After much trial and error, I settled on a simple strategy. Work first and most extensively with those functional and operational leaders who are eager to work with you. You will discover some who are enthusiastic about learning the implications of security and who will welcome your visit to their facilities to learn about workplace violence or other concerns. Now is the time to wear your marketing hat.

Whomever you decide to approach, keep it simple. Internal staff have been cut to the bone and are already overworked. One of the ways I have been successful at getting senior management to enhance security is to make obvious the advantages of a given security initiative. Let's take fraud prevention program; this can deliver straightforward and positive business results in terms of dollars recovered and demonstrate to employees that fraudulent behavior is not a part of business ethics or values.

Some departments, such as audit, don't have many opportunities to do anything creative that potentially has broad benefits for the business. Overcome initial resistance by designing a simple assessment and prevention tool—a one-page program. List the purpose of fraud prevention, and follow with five to seven questions. Finish the page noting the desired outcomes.

I suggest that before you begin such a program, you have casual conversations with leaders in accounting, audit, finance, and purchasing departments. Find out which leaders are most receptive, and begin there. It may be possible to start with one or two simple pilot programs across select segments of the business. This will get you working with people in their departments and ironing out kinks as they arise. We have worked with and helped many efforts succeed; they are cost-effective; they enhance teamwork; and sometimes they unearth surprisingly positive business outcomes.

In the past, security leaders struggled to find ways to communicate the importance of genuine security to the business. Sometimes we were at the mercy of finance and operations analysts who could demonstrate, at budget time, that the dollars invested in security would be better spent to increase sales or improve production times.

Fortunately, today there are meaningful measures and metrics that will help you to identify the business value of security. For example, there is *Measures and Metrics in Corporate Security: A Workbook for Demonstrating How Security Adds Value to Business* by George Campbell. This book is a boon to the security professional in identifying what should be measured for virtually any business or organization. There are over 350 metrics in 13 categories. Smart senior security leaders will tailor this valuable reference often to deliver ever improving business results. Why measure? For the good reason that often, "what gets measured, gets done."

Simply exploring the use and misuse of security vendors is an immensely practical approach. Often it is one of the most fruitful ways to reintegrate security to deliver better results, financial and otherwise, for the business. For example, many organizations lose major funds when they do not have the expertise to evaluate or question, let alone rely on, the advice of vendors or facility management firms for major security system investments.

One company purchased a "new" security system in the early 1990s. The vendor doing a presentation, on behalf of a facility management firm, had assured the approving finance team that the system would meet their needs into the foreseeable future. The cost was $1,300,000.

Unfortunately, it was an analog system that had been designed in the 1970s using technology developed in the 1960s. In just a few years, the system was not able to deal with the overcapacity and went obsolete. Spare parts for the system were unavailable and it was seriously outdated and security was being compromised on a daily basis. Not only that the business could not get the full advantage to depreciate their investment but also was a total loss. The digital system that replaced it had been available when the analog system was installed; it had unlimited capacity and used universally available replacement parts. It cost less than half the price of its predecessor.

The same vigilance must be applied to outsourcing security contracts, for example, for security guards. If a contract is in place for 10 years, with automatic increases of 3% yearly, and no one has time to review such "bargains," they turn into major financial drains for the business. A security leader who knows her or his business can spot such inefficiencies with relative ease.

A security professional can also understand, and help executives to realize, the true cost of theft, fraud, and other business losses. For example, 85% of thefts are internal; they are committed by employees or contractors.

I vividly remember the first time we presented an overview of general fraud issues and the importance of an effective fraud prevention program to corporate executives shortly after I had joined the company as their security leader. There was a subtle undertone of disbelief. There were a few indirect remarks and snickers at the beginning of the presentation. After all, embezzlement was not part of the curriculum at the MBA level. When a presenter discusses methods of committing fraud, most people don't know how to react; the subject makes them nervous.

The side comments and snickers were an indicator, albeit a negative one, that the audience was paying attention. "Humor, particularly dark humor, is a common way to communicate true concern ... with this type of humor, an idea comes into consciousness that, in context, seems as outlandish as to be ridiculous. And that's precisely why it's funny. The point is, though, that the idea came into consciousness. Why? Because all the information was there" (see *The Gift of Fear* by Gavin de Becker, pp. 84–87).

If a presenter is surprised and taken aback by dark humor he or she can be thrown off track and allow it to disrupt a presentation. So at that point, I outlined some financial information on the subject of fraud. A national study at the time indicated that US organizations were losing about 7% of their annual revenue to fraud (The Wells Report, 1996, ACFE). Our corporation's net earnings after tax (NEAT) for the preceding year were less than 2%. Needless to say I had everyone's attention. Several of those in the room challenged the figures.

However, we were now ready for the real dialogue. I noted that there seemed to be a disagreement that 7% of our annual revenues could be lost to fraud. I continued: since I am the new guy on the block, let's cut that figure in half. Perhaps fraud is only costing us 3.5%. Again, there were further objections. So, I said OK, let's cut that figure in half again, to 1.75%. Now, perhaps you think that's still too much, so let's assume that we lose only 8/10 of 1% of our gross revenue to fraudulent activities or theft.

If we are collectively smart, and can trim down losses, frauds, embezzlements, and thefts to 8/10 of 1%, we will add $40,000,000 to our net income (NI) or NEAT and to the bottom line. That's what I want to do. I want to work with each one of you to figure out how we can add profit margin to each of your business units.

I continued, "if our combined operations are losing $40,000,000 (8/10 of 1%) or $80,000,000, (1.75%) or, even worse, $160,000,000 (3.5%) to fraud or theft, we all have to work a lot harder or the business could possibly go under. But I am impressed with the organization's work ethic and prefer to work with you and contribute to your success."

The security function has but two simple goals for any business: make the workplace safe for its employees and enable the business to keep the money it has earned. At the end of each fiscal quarter, our marching orders are not about how many sales we made, or products we manufactured, or about the efficiency of our various distribution platforms and systems. Rather, the aim for each and every business segment was for them to meet their NEAT revenue targets.

There was a long pause. I waited. Everyone was quiet; they had listened. From then on we looked forward to the challenge of delivering meaningful security practices as part of the business and contributing to its financial success. From that point on, the only "snickers" came in brown wrappers.

There was an atmosphere of relaxed camaraderie as we left the room; the time was well spent. Moving forward, corporate security in that company was accepted in a new way. Leaders had heard that I was prepared to work alongside them. Some of the relationships established in that room continue to this day.

A fraud prevention approach works well in departments that have routine contact with core business functions. For example, our audit department determined how best to review vendor accounts. Word quickly spread through the organization's purchasing departments that "audit was in here and reviewed every aspect of our entire vendor establishment process." Such opportunities truly enhance business results.

If audit or finance departments think you are out for your own glory, you will encounter resistance. Whatever programs are crafted must be created in collaboration with business units, with their needs in mind. Security goals must be completely open, transparent, and subject to critique by those with whom you are working. Your success is secondary to their success and the success of the business.

Here are some important objectives to consider. First, if there is an ethics program, work with them to incorporate a strong approach to fraud/theft awareness and prevention across the organization.

Build the program on existing staff infrastructure and do it in a way that adds little or no work to what they are already tasked to do. Have member of the field audit team work with the security team in designing the outcomes and results you are looking for. This sends the message that the business has established expectations and values that apply to everyone—employees, contractors, vendors, and executives.

Second, the security leader needs the direct support of executive management to legally pursue, either civilly or criminally, all issues of theft and fraud above a predetermined threshold with the objective to achieve maximum financial recovery.

Many years ago, I looked for a way to put in plain words the real impact that theft was having on one company. What evolved was a straightforward business math formula, coupled with a very conservative multiple factor when the loss was the result of fraud or embezzlement. To demonstrate the impact, I decided to show what it takes for a business to make a true profit of $1,000 when the NEAT was only 1.6%. At that level, it takes $62,500 worth of organizational effort (manufacturing, distribution, consulting, or other revenue sources) to have $1,000 in NI or NEAT "fall" to the bottom line.

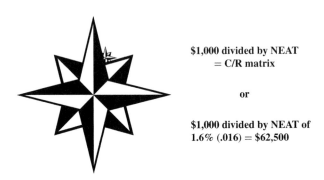

$1,000 divided by NEAT
= C/R matrix

or

$1,000 divided by NEAT of
1.6% (.016) = $62,500

Quilter's cost/recovery matrix or Q-CRM. Copyright 2006 Q Solutions, LLC. All Rights Reserved.

The most fundamental business figure at the end of the fiscal year is the NI or NEAT, the profit after everything has been paid—raw materials, facilities, manufacturing, employees, and, of course, taxes. The higher the NEAT percentage, the less effort the organization must expend to reach a given profit goal.

Let's illustrate this reality further. If NEAT for a given business is 7%, it will take $14,286 in organizational effort to generate that same $1,000 in pure profit or NEAT. If the NEAT is 2.7%, the organization must expend $37,037 in costly effort to realize a profit of $1,000. If, in the course of a fiscal year, a business sustains a $1,000 loss for which they can account, such as theft of inventory, then the business recognizes that as a direct loss. The $37,037 in organizational effort added exactly zero to the bottom line.

However, if the loss involves fraud or embezzlement, losses are often harder to detect. "It is recognized that these cases may go undetected for years before they are caught" (Report to the Nation on Occupational Fraud and Abuse, 2006, p. 8, ACFE).

In thinking through the above Q-CRM process with several financial leaders, our consensus was to be conservative and simply use a multiple of 2 years to represent the time it would take to detect and stop an embezzlement. If such a crime is discovered in an organization with a 7% NEAT profit goal, there is justification to identify that loss as twice $14,286 or $28,572 for every $1,000 that did not make it to the bottom line.

This dynamic is illustrated in the chart below. The chart reflects two important realities. First, it demonstrates what it takes for the organization to make a NEAT profit. Second, it demonstrates how damaging fraud and embezzlement are to the firm's bottom line, because of the multiple factor. So when $5,000 does not make it to the NEAT line because of fraud, the sales effort to recover that amount is $370,370 (2 × $185,185). A $50,000 loss escalates to $3,703,704 (2 × $1,851,852).

The Cost of Fraud/Embezzlement to a Business with a 2.7% NEAT		
NEAT/NI Loss	Overachievement Revenue Needed to Recover	Fraud/Embezzlement 2 × Factor
$1,000	$37,037	$74,074
$5,000	$185,185	$370,370
$25,000	$925,925	$1,851,850
$50,000	$1,851,850	$3,703,700
$75,000	$2,777,775	$5,555,550
$100,00	$3,703,700	$7,407,400

This information illustrates how important it is for the security team to communicate the significance of losses due to fraud in business terms. It also shows how imperative it is to directly relate security efforts to the specific operating plans of individual business segments. To do this effectively, you and the core members of the security team must already have established solid relationships with the leadership teams of each aspect of the business.

Consider the business impact of the information above in light of recent research. Each year, the ACFE issues a concise summary in its "Report to the Nation on Occupational Fraud and Abuse." This document includes a two-page summary report which should be shared with business leaders. Here are a few highlights from the 2006 summary:

- Fraud costs US organizations 5% of their annual revenue.
- Fraud schemes are more likely to be detected by a tip than by other means, such as internal or external audits or controls.
- Most schemes involve either the accounting department or upper management.
- Less than 8% of perpetrators had prior convictions.
- The size of the loss caused by fraud is related to the position of the perpetrator.
- The last point is significant. Perpetrators with 5–10 years of service accounted for 26% of all cases with a median loss of over $200,000. Employees with over 10 years of service accounted for almost 36% of all cases, with a median loss of over $260,000.

I use a mantra to help me to communicate this point to business leaders. It is not what the business earns that is important ... rather it's what the business keeps.

Security leaders must think and act proactively to protect not only the hard assets of a business but also its revenue. Security is actually in a unique position to enhance the profit margin of a business, and to participate in its financial success. And you do not need to focus on the entire organization to save it from most cases of major fraud: focus on accounting and upper management, because most fraud happens there—51% of all cases with median losses of $199,000 and $900,000, respectively. In addition, the purchasing department, which accounted for only 3% of the cases, had a median loss of $1,000,000.

An article in *The Wall Street Journal* by James Kelly and Scott Nadler, titled "Leading from Below," makes interesting points about what it takes to be a business leader below the C-suite level. In light of this chapter, I share the key points of their article:

- Make the decision to be a leader.
- Focus on influence, not control.
- Make your mental organizational chart horizontal rather than vertical.
- Work on your "trusted advisor" skills.
- Don't wait for the perfect time to initiate action; just find a good time.

Kelly and Nadler summarize many of the choices that I have made as a security leader in several businesses. Is it easy? No, it is not. Does such leadership make a difference? You bet it does. It makes your organization more profitable as well as more secure; it reframes everything you propose and do for your business. Such high-quality leadership positions the security principal for greater acceptance and results. It benefits everyone.

CHAPTER 8

Companions on the Journey

No man is an island.

John Donne

I grew up around athletes. The sound of basketballs pounding asphalt, or of tennis balls whizzing through the air, were among the sounds of home. My dad had friends who were world-class baseball and basketball players. A certain kind of teamwork was also part of our family culture. We all took part in various kinds of work, play, and caring for one another. This was part of my formation to teamwork. As an adult, I have also coached teams; this has been one of my joys as a parent.

In a professional setting, when the right people come together to achieve a worthwhile goal, the outcomes are wonderful. This is true in medical research, in manufacturing, in global logistics, and in education. When the right skills, the right approach, and the right disciplines are aligned with the right individuals, their collaboration is a joy to watch. It can become a form of play. A great team motivated to accomplish a specific goal moves with a level of energy, respect, and excitement that is comparable to the beauty in motion and zest in performance of Olympic athletes.

In the work of security leadership, much of your success depends on building strong, trusting internal relationships. At the very heart of this enterprise is building a core security team. Finally, you and your team must network; you must continually enhance your learning and relationships with trusted security colleagues. No one becomes a true security leader in splendid isolation. Teamwork is absolutely essential to your effectiveness as well as your perseverance in such a demanding role.

In this chapter, I will discuss the goal of teamwork; its guiding principles; how to be the right leader for the right team; positioning the team within the larger collaborative structures of the business; the significance of cross-functional teams; the security leader as player-coach; hiring the right team; mentoring your team; celebrating the expertise of an excellent team player; and sending that player on to new challenges.

8.1 THE DEFINITION OF CORE SECURITY TEAM

The core security team is a nucleus of talented security professionals who have the expertise, knowledge, skill, ability, drive, know-how, and desire to address any kind of security issue or risk that may touch a company's employees, information (digital or traditional), finances, property, systems, facilities, or brands. They also have the ability to enhance one another's gifts by working smoothly together.

8.2 THE RIGHT LEADER FOR THE RIGHT TEAM

We have all been on teams that just never gelled or that fell apart. The composition of a team is often a determining factor in the success of a project. Many teams never meet their stated objectives. Executives must find the right person to lead a security team.

In today's business environment, this is a significant undertaking if the business is to have any hope of delivering meaningful security, that is, security that is both sustainable and profitable for the business.

In order to hire the right security manager, director of security, chief security officer (CSO), or whatever the organization calls its security leader executives, they need to have a clear vision of the primary tasks of that person. If not, the new security leader needs to be confident and prepared to help the executives understand the scope of those responsibilities. Depending on how well the scope of the job is worked out, applied, and adapted will have a significant impact on what is or is not accomplished.

It is imperative for the security leader to present the full spectrum of security skills and how they will be tailored to meet identified security risks in the business. By addressing these issues up front, business and the security leader will better understand ways that security can drive business results in collaboration with senior leaders and their teams. The previous chapters will have helped you to flesh out the meaning of this statement.

8.3 THE GOAL OF THE CORE SECURITY TEAM

The goal of the core security team is to work across all levels of management to resolve every kind of security issue. When an excellent team is in place, this is fun because it helps the business to become more productive. When leaders at all levels come to know and trust you, you can work not only quickly but also effectively together. With the right corporate culture supporting you, your team greatly enhances the business goals in "a company of winners."

8.4 HIRING THE RIGHT CORE TEAM

Perhaps the first organization you join may have some security leader or a security team in place. While this may have some advantages, it usually has significant drawbacks. I actually prefer to build a team from the ground up. Think of Ralph, Picasso, and Dorothy as examples described in earlier chapters and you will understand why.

The security leader is responsible for ensuring that those who make up the core team have the skills, maturity, flexibility, and capacity for cooperation to work well together. It is a huge challenge to find, develop, and maintain a team with just the right chemistry. In conversations with colleagues who have successfully transitioned from public to private sector, many have noted that hiring the right team members was not only difficult but also represented a huge adjustment.

Why is finding the right hires such a demanding task? Often in the public sector, leaders have had the benefit of choosing people from best qualified lists. These candidates have spent many years competing in the same organization—a police department, government agency, or branch of the military service—where both the candidate and the leader shared a common culture and had clear expectations about what the new opportunity meant. Those who have been successful public sector leaders may trip-up because they select someone with the right skills but overlook issues such as generational gaps when it comes to work habits, loyalty, or job expectations.

When hiring, it is wise to build on the already existing foundation in your business culture. Think of it like this: if your administrative team is looking for new office space, they will search the market for an appropriate building to purchase or rent—one that fits the needs of their business precisely. They won't buy a piece of land and start digging holes. That would be both time consuming and expensive.

When you are considering building a security team, seek out other teams in your organization that are known to be really great at achieving cross-functional results. Ask a cross-functional facilitator for that team, or perhaps the primary leader, if you may sit in on a few sessions and listen to how they handle key issues. Make sure you make it clear that your intention is to listen and learn and that everything you hear will be strictly confidential. After all you are seeking to understand how cross-functional techniques work within their business and how best to achieve results. If you are lucky, you may find several examples of solid cross-functional efforts in your organization. If this is not the case, you may need to reach out to other organizations.

Taking time to do this will accelerate your learning about the culture of the business, and how existing teams manage their tasks, or struggle to, in your organization. Let it be known that you are there for one reason: to listen, listen, listen, and nothing else.

There is no room for an average or partially satisfactory performance (grade C) on a core security team. In fact, there is little room for above-average performance (grade B). In building a great team, you are seeking out exceptional and outstanding players (grade A). These individuals have a mix of motivation and skills that complement the needs of the business. They also must have balance in their life that facilitates their ability to lead. These are common-sense criteria.

When hiring:

- Take the time to hire individuals with solid values.
- Seek out those who already know how to work hard.
- Search for those who respect everyone with whom they come in contact, those who have already polished their personal and team business skills.
- Find enthusiastic, intelligent, high-energy individuals who crave to make a difference every day.
- Seek those whose skills are diverse enough to complement those of other teammates.
- Look for those who can maintain trust; not doing so can have ominous consequences for security.
- Look for lifelong learners.
- Be patient. Find individuals who believe in concepts similar to "We must give more than we get and leave more than we take."
- Hire those who will enhance both the ethics and the success of the organization.

Imagine you get a call from an executive or a manager and she says she needs your help now for an important security issue. If you don't have a team, you are the one who will respond. If you have developed a team with bench strength, then you have the flexibility of being able to call on several different security team members and you have the confidence that they will make the right things happen at the right time.

Timely and effective resolution of security issues for the business is the mission of your team. Every time you work well toward this end, the stock of your entire team goes up. Life gets easier.

8.5 NECESSARY ATTRIBUTES OF CORE SECURITY TEAMS

In their book, *Teamwork: What Must Go Right/What Can Go Wrong* by Carl E. Larson and Frank M. J. LaFasto, the authors describe Problem-Resolution Teams, Creative Teams, and Tactical Teams, and the attributes of each type of successful team. Core security teams that we have developed have needed a mix of each of these team concepts. Though they are the businesses's security teams, they must have the strength, structure, and flexibility of a cross-functional team with most of the qualities described below:

1. Problem-Resolution Teams: "The first broad team objective ... is to resolve problems in an ongoing basis. When this is the broad purpose of the collective team effort, the most important and necessary feature of the team is TRUST. Each member of the team must expect and believe the interactions among members will be truthful and embody a high degree of integrity. Each member must believe that the team will be fairly consistent and mature in its approach to dealing with problems.
2. Creative Teams: A second broad objective of a team is "to create something" and a necessary feature of the structure of the team is autonomy. The process focus for the creative team is that of exploring possibilities and alternatives. For a creative team to function, it is necessary to have autonomy from the systems and procedures, as well as to create an atmosphere in which ideas do not become prematurely quashed.
3. Tactical Teams: The third broad team objective is to execute a well-defined plan. This broad-brush objective is most notably characterized by clarity. For tactical teams to be successful, there must be high task clarity and unambiguous role definition. Consider the examples of a cardiac surgical team and the crew of an aircraft carrier. The success of each of these teams depends upon a high degree of responsiveness from team members, a high degree of clarity in terms of who does what, and a clear set of performance standards.

As security leaders—every member of the core team is a leader—we need to display the levels of trust, autonomy, and clarity described above in order to bring about problem resolution using creative approaches and producing tactical results if we are to successfully achieve a sound security environment across a large corporation.

8.6 CROSS-FUNCTIONAL TEAMS

In another of their works *When Teams Work Best* by Frank LaFasto and Carl Larson (pp. 90–92), the authors discuss the opinions of 6,000 team members and leaders who describe what it takes to succeed. Among their findings is a discussion of the realities of how cross-functional teams come together to solve problems, as well as the challenges presented by membership in such a team. A few findings are presented below:

> *Though cross-functional teams bring breadth of perspective and expertise, they also bring fragmented loyalties, divided time commitments, and even conflicting demands. In cross-functional teams, both substantive and process problems become intensified. When a large and very complex organization redirects or refocuses its efforts, many changes may be made. Such changes usually require a cross-functional team approach. You may not think that cross-functional team members, all of whom work for the same organization and pursue, theoretically, the same goals, would have much trouble working together. But they do. With cross-functional teams, the problems are big, broad problems, and clarity is difficult to achieve.*
>
> *Although these challenges are formidable, there is a way forward that pointed to the importance of kicking around the problem before trying to solve it. The principle, in a nutshell, is that the more the problem is large, complex, and has multiple perspectives, the more important it is not to talk about solutions too early in the process. Rather, spend considerable time talking about the interests they have in trying to solve the problem, experiences they've had with similar kinds of problems, etc. Far from being a waste of time, this early informal exploring helps overcome much of the cynicism or mistrust that may drive the discussion off-track in the future.*

8.7 THE PLAYER-COACH

In building a security team I enjoy using basketball as a model. I have been influenced by the work of two great coaches: John Wooden and Phil Jackson. Although they coached at different levels but dealt with issues unique to college and professional players, they share key perspectives and values for the talent they coached: hard work, keeping one's head in the game, developing solid skills in both defense and offense, and accountability to the team. As a result, they took talented players and fashioned legendary teams. I highly recommend any one of the many books written by either of these coaches.

In working with a security team, I strive to be a player-coach. First, I seek to understand what it will take to accomplish and exceed expectations. Once I am familiar with the tasks and the business environment, I look for people who are thoroughgoing professionals, who are looking for the right opportunity, and who have the will to excel.

8.8 CHARACTERISTICS OF THE PLAYER-COACH

8.8.1 Strategist

A player-coach is first of all a strategist. He looks at the big picture and then figures out whatever might go wrong in the game. For example, in security, I like to list who in the organization should be the first to know if:

- Sensitive business information is stolen.
- A bomb threat occurs.
- There is a break-in at an off-site warehouse.
- An accident that involves employees.
- Someone is injured on company property.
- A major fraud is suspected.
- There is a possibility for serious workplace violence.

This is just the beginning of such a list. Once the list is made, I initiate introductory calls to executives in the functional areas that would handle such incidents and ask to see them at their convenience. Learning by walking around helps me to begin to develop a reality-based strategy. It is not wise to assume that I know who should be the first to know.

A good strategist also knows how to forewarn and thus forearm his or her business team. When I was in government service, we had one field division that chewed up one new management team after another. I was in headquarters and involved in helping to select members of such teams—those folks with proven track records who knew how to get things done. For a few years in succession, we sent bright and talented leaders into that field division and after a year they would be worn to a frazzle. The changes they were to accomplish were blocked by a stubborn and entrenched workforce.

Finally, we took a step back at headquarters and did a careful assessment of the culture of this field division. Then we brought together a new management team and through discussion, armed them with awareness of the realities they would be facing. This research and analysis empowered them to meet the challenge in a new way.

As a result, within a year they were able to achieve meaningful change that totally turned around the field division. The improvements they initiated have enhanced the work of that division for over 20 years. This experience has many applications for teamwork in the business world. If you are moving from the public sector to the private sector, reflect on your own learning experiences and be prepared to translate them in the new culture.

Perhaps, the primary attribute of an excellent strategist is good judgment. No matter what kind of background you have, or how strong your professional or business skills are, real success always depends on good judgment. How we exercise judgment throughout life, what we choose to do or not do, has a cumulative effect on how we reach judgments when we are under pressure.

Such judgments determine the value of the results we produce. It does not make any difference if we are dealing with organizations or individuals. The ability to exercise sound judgment is as essential to successful business as offense and defense are to a basketball team.

"With good judgment, little else matters." This is a key premise in the book *Judgment: How Winning Leaders Make Great Calls* by Noel M. Tichy and Warren G. Bennis.

Their work focuses on three domains and how individuals make informed decisions within these areas:

1. Judgments about people.
2. Judgments about strategy.
3. Judgments in times of crisis.

Tichy and Bennis describe these domains as being influenced by how a leader prepares to make important decisions, when they "make a call," how they make it succeed, and finally, once the decision is "executed" what they do to ensure that a decision achieves "the desired results."

The preparation to make a call and how it is executed is dependent on four areas of knowledge:

1. About oneself.
2. About the involvement of social networks.

3. About the organization.
4. About the context of the decision.

While I think that leaders of all kinds will benefit from this book, it has special significance for security leaders. One of the key points that Tichy and Bennis make is: "strategy matters, but forming the team matters more."

The decisions security leaders make, or fail to make, can have far-reaching human and organizational consequences. These decisions will either facilitate or impede the outcomes and consequences for employees and the business. The security leader and his or her core team must be well prepared and have the confidence of the organization's leaders long before a serious incident or crisis starts to develop. If this has been achieved then, as an incident starts to unfold, the security team will have the confidence and support they need in order to focus on the seamless implementation of whatever actions are required to resolve issues ethically and in ways that truly benefits the business.

8.8.2 Well Positioned to Lead

The player-coach needs an accurate sense of where his or her work begins and ends. As a security leader, such a coach needs a strong network of peers beyond the corporation, and a clearly worked out understanding of his or her exact role and authority within the corporation. The security leader and in fact all the core security team members— since they are all leaders—will know or need to know or resolve answers to the following questions:

- What are your precise tasks? Do you lead or do you just manage security?
- Does the scope of your position include all aspects of security risk— people, information, facilities, reputation, systems—or just some of the above?
- What is the span of your responsibility, accountability, and authority?
- Do you have control over who is on your team?
- When major security issues surface, will senior business leaders seek and listen for your recommendations, or do they or others preempt your input and decide how the issue will be resolved?

These are not ego-related questions. Rather, they clarify your position, and thus the potential strength of your team, in essential ways. Security is a team effort. If you believe you have a really sound solution to a security issue, you need to discuss it with a number of other stakeholders; they probably have some excellent input. The solution for the business is enhanced by the shared wisdom of those most directly involved, as well as those charged with leadership.

Some executives realize that security will have unique access to business planning, decision making, sensitive information, as well as most of the problems across the organization. In the past, corporate leaders wanted as little as possible to do with security; since post-9/11, all that has changed. Occasionally, you may find an executive who wants to exert total control in this area. Although this is rare, you may need to deal with such a person, especially if your company is being acquired by another corporation.

Most veteran business leaders will determine the level of access they are willing to give their security leader, at least in general terms. The degree of access you have indicates volumes about the management philosophy on which a particular business culture operates. In some organizations, there is very open sharing; executives may expect the security leader to function in the same way.

However, this level of openness may at first be disconcerting to a security leader from the public sector whose history and experience of sharing information is highly restrictive. For example, in highly compartmentalized government operations, information sharing was on a strictly "need to know" basis. If your prior experience was in public service, be prepared for a cultural change.

Organizations with a high degree of openness are often very creative, flexible, and swift in decision making. This usually works well in their business operations. Occasionally, organizational openness may conflict with security needs. As each security activity, investigation, or review is different, it is always best to have the appropriate executive identify who should have access; who should be briefed. Be proactive about approaching executives with such decisions. It is not only necessary in some instances but also gives you further contact with business leaders and enhances trust.

Routine time with executives gives them an opportunity to see how you handle a variety of security challenges across the business when done well. It also proves your worth to those in C-level positions. As you build trust in the position of security leader, you are laying the foundations for corporate trust in a core security team.

8.8.3 Lifelong Learner/Teacher

A good security leader, like a good coach, learns from everyone, from every experience, from success and from failure, from books and from life. You will never achieve this kind of holistic grasp of "the game" by sitting in an office. Every environment has its own security challenges. Energy platforms in the Gulf of Mexico, manufacturing plants in Thailand, million-square-foot distribution centers, inner-city bill-paying centers share one constant—they all have employees.

Learning what and how they contribute to the business builds your business acumen. Someone who is as eager to learn as well as to coach usually has excellent instincts for succession planning through the careful selection of team members. Those who will remain after you are gone, if well coached, will continue to make security a core resource for the business—a resource solidly built into its culture.

8.8.4 Commitment, Encouragement, and Toughness

A leader focused on building great teams will spend most of his or her time being a tough coach. Tough does not necessarily mean rough. It means demanding and consistent—with a capacity for empathy at the right moments. Above all, it means leading by example. In the past, I have worked with team members who faced huge challenges and needed help to move in new directions. Some were alcoholics, but because they chose the difficult path to recovery and had the support of others, including their coach, they were able to turn their lives around. Others may have needed polishing—although they appeared to be chunks of coal on the outside, there were diamonds waiting to be discovered within; they began to shine.

LaFasto and Larson (*Teamwork*) describe their study on the topic of teamwork: "The logic that emerged from our research regarding how important encouragement and support is to decision making is simple and difficult to ignore:

- To achieve an elevated goal or vision, change must occur.
- For change to occur, a decision must be made.

- For a decision to occur, a choice must be made.
- To make a choice, a risk must be taken.
- To encourage risk taking, a supportive climate must exist.
- A supportive climate is demonstrated by day-to-day leadership behavior."

Your day-to-day leadership behavior with your core security team, and beyond it, in collaborating with corporate leaders, creates "multiplier effects," which can lead to excellent business results. Business leaders are accustomed to dealing with a wide range of business risks. The security leader's experience and know-how, magnified by the coordinated expertise of an excellent core security team, simply helps the business deal even more effectively with various domains of risk.

If there is a simple formula for demonstrating day-to-day leadership behavior, it is to be a committed, tough, and encouraging player-coach for your core security team. This kind of commitment involves constant reflection about how you and your team can better mitigate risk for your company.

As a coach, you require much of yourself and those working with you. You encourage, help them to acquire meaningful professional credentials, demand verifiable business results and demonstrate how to attain them, and advocate progressively more challenging assignments and programs to advance their leadership skills in a business environment. Perhaps you make it possible for them to earn advanced degrees. Time spent in such endeavors pays handsome dividends.

8.8.5 Flexibility

Just as being a player-coach takes physical and mental agility and flexibility, being in a parallel position as a security leader requires the ability to respond quickly to unique opportunities and challenges. Organizations today are in constant transition. The security leader of today and tomorrow must be capable of succeeding in any domestic or global environment. This takes energy, intelligence, commitment, and courage.

Members of your team learn what leadership takes by seeing it modeled and doing security tasks together. Today's executives know that strong team collaboration is a force multiplier in delivering innovative business results.

8.8.6 Trust

As LaFasto and Larson explain in *Teamwork*:

> *Trust improves the quality of collaborative efforts because with it, decisions are more intone with what is in fact happening. Problems are raised and dealt with instead of hidden until they become disastrous. People are willing to try something because there's a chance that it might work rather than remain inactive because of their fear of failure. And if something internal to the team itself is interfering with the team's success, then that problem is more likely to be confronted and resolved.*
>
> *Trust leads to compensating. One explanation that has been offered for why teams sometimes succeed—even beyond reasonable explanations for success—is that "compensating" arises. Compensation happens when one team member picks up the slack that occurs when another member falters. If a lot of compensation occurs, then a whole team is capable of pulling itself, collectively, to new levels of performance.*

It is good to know that the importance of a constant theme of this book—earning and building trust at all levels of the business endeavor—is substantiated by solid research. The best corporations in the world understand this. That is why they are great places to work.

8.8.7 Leader with High Expectations

Once the right team is on board, this is what the leader can and should expect of each of his professionals:

- Everyone is to do their best at all times, on and off the court.
- Each has unique skills and abilities. All are needed to make this the best team ever.
- All of us will be in and maintain top physical and mental shape.
- We pay attention to the game (the business) at all times.
- We are lifelong learners.
- Everyone gets to play. Before we hit the court, there will be extensive practice:
  - We all rebound and move the ball up the floor.
  - We run, pass, make assists, and when we can, we score for the business.
  - We play defense as a team.
  - We adjust, move, and flex as we keep our eyes on those we are defending—employees first, then business assets.
  - Everyone gets to make decisions on the floor.
  - We will inevitably make mistakes.

- All decisions must be made with right intent.
- We will all learn from every decision.

Senior business leaders at all levels who are new to dealing with the new security paradigm relate well to the basketball analogy. It also helps them to realize that you are reflecting on the business and that you relate to business issues and that security is there to deliver meaningful results.

Once those chosen for the team commit to being the best, they must prove their worth. Once proven, they earn the distinction of being "The A team."

My focus in working with the members is to begin as the player-coach. They know I am available to them 24/7. As core team members understand their role and its impact, they gradually take over more decision making. Each of us "is the team," and we rely on the advice, skills, knowledge, and backup of all its members.

Once a high level of trust is established, team members share more and more of their challenges. In doing so, each grows in confidence. The team becomes more resilient, as well as more capable of serving the organization.

With the exception of my first corporate gig, as an outsourced director of security, I was able to build strong internal security teams which outlived me. In every instance, it was my choice when I left each of these businesses. I never left without ensuring that an "A" team was in place to carry on security leadership.

8.9 MENTORING TALENTED TEAM MEMBERS: SENDING THEM ON THEIR WAY

Someone has said that to be a good teacher, you must give the next generation roots and wings. I believe the same is true of the player-coach. When a member of a successful team chooses to move on, it is usually for a good reason. Sometimes life directions change; perhaps they have matured to a point where they need a new challenge or they would like to test themselves as the leader. Perhaps they want experience in a different industry or organization. They are ready. They launch.

What prepared them for new horizons? I believe most of them would say that their security careers gave them the opportunity to grow both personally and professionally. Above all, they are business savvy.

Tony came on board our team as a new security manager. Aside from time in the military, he had just a few months of security management experience at that time. However, he displayed tremendous poise, work ethic, and desire to learn everything he could about business and security. He became a Certified Protection Professional (CPP) within months. We worked together for just over 3 years.

When our company was acquired, he was promoted and became a director, which made him my peer. We were two of four directors reporting to a vice president of a sixty billion dollar business. A few years later Tony was recruited by another huge enterprise, but this time it was a privately held business and he was their first senior security leader and global security director.

This time, he was asked to build security for the corporation from the ground up and to recruit a team in the process. Eventually he was recruited away from this firm; he left one of his recruits to succeed him. Currently, he is the head of security for a global consumer business with operations on five continents and a global security team.

Marsha was hired as a security coordinator. Although she had worked with law enforcement, she had no formal business security background. She came with outstanding recommendations, was bilingual, worked independently, and was eager to learn everything about security. As a member of our original business team, she stepped up to every challenge. She also went on to earn her CPP. When her life situation changed, she eventually started her own security consulting practice. Today she is a security manager for a well-known computer company.

Joe was hired as a security manager to replace Tony when he was promoted. Previously, Joe had been a senior account executive with a national security provider. He was very bright and already had his CPP. When I was recruited to join another business, Joe's credentials and experience were so strong that he was promoted to replace me as security director. Within a few years, he became vice president of physical security for the parent company. Today he has moved on and is now the vice president of investigations for a Fortune 20 company.

Leo was the first person I hired after I was recruited to build a new security program for a major energy provider. He had extensive experience with a number of technologies. Leo came to my attention through a colleague who knew him well and held him in high esteem. Although he lacked a college degree, Leo had excellent people skills and was very quick to learn the business operations he supported. Eager to prove himself, he is on track to earn his degree.

Larry was different. Although had no business security experience when I interviewed him, he had superb investigative skills; he had been Resident Agent in Charge for a federal law enforcement agency. His goal was to learn corporate security. Today, Larry is the security manager of several different business units across a number of states.

Uniquely, Gerald had been part of the business for close to 30 years. He had extensive hands-on experience in every operational aspect of the company. Educated as a professional engineer, his first security experience began with preparations for Y2K. When 9/11 occurred, his business leaders made him the CSO for a segment of the business. For some time, he continued to report to his business unit until the company decided to make him a member of our corporate security team. He earned his CPP in record time. When it was time for me to move on, I was very pleased when Gerald was selected to succeed me as senior security leader for the business.

My purpose in sharing snapshots of these coworkers is that they came to a security team with diverse backgrounds and life experiences. Their personal and professional success is a reflection of their individual gifts; but they showed up, worked hard every day, learned the business, and were honest about their strengths and weaknesses. All enjoyed being members of a team where they could grow, make mistakes, and learn from them. Each was committed to making a positive impact with every task.

More than ever, businesses need the total security leader. These leaders are capable of dealing with every kind of security challenge and contingency faced by large corporations.

Reflecting on the growth of my former teammates brings me great satisfaction because of the work they have done, the difference they have made, and the privilege of working with them on the same team. I am proud of them and of the work we continue together.

CHAPTER *9*

Moving Toward the Destination

In this chapter, I will review what I hope you will take away from this book.

Being the head of security for a business or NGO takes considerable experience, a high level of flexibility, and a willingness to not only work with but also work on behalf of employees and the organization. Your job is to bring all of your knowledge, skills, and abilities to enhance the safety and security of the employees and the enterprise. To achieve this takes equal parts of caring, creativity, and commitment.

When someone steps out of a very successful first career in the public sector and into a second career in private industry, especially in the field of security, I believe it should mean only one thing: you really care about people. Close behind that goal is making a positive impact for the business. Taking care of employees and producing business results in any organization take long hours and lots of patience.

Learn the business first. You must know it before you can assess it. Then determine its security needs in light of the business culture and requirements. Keep your messages and most especially your PowerPoint slides simple, direct, and focused on what is really needed, not on what you would prefer to have.

In more than 15 years in the corporate security field, this is what I have learned:

Be brilliant on the basics. Know the building blocks of the security profession. Establish a team that has no hierarchy and be willing to be both a player and a coach. Join ASIS and CSI to grow and stay current with your expertise. If you are in larger organizations and eligible, consider joining ISMA or the SEC.

Seek expert guides. Develop relationships with other professionals. You will find they not only understand but also will share perspective, information, and the expertise of a lifetime. Many have a wide breadth of experience in fields beyond the traditional disciplines of security including HR, academics, research, and technical gurus. Seek out consultants. Ask fellow security leaders whom they depend on when they are stumped. Stay in touch with your network two or three times a year. They will help you with the challenges you face and will coach you through really hard times. Well-built relationships last a lifetime.

Know the territory. Culture is the DNA of the business. The culture of the business will give you the perspective that is needed to create both the security strategy and programs that will be initially accepted and which can then be sustained over many years. Developing a strategy based on a business culture ensures sustainability even as the business adapts and changes to reflect customer needs and the products or services it provides. Usually the culture of a business outlasts management and even product changes, so build your effort on something that lasts.

Travel in good company. This sounds easy but it's not. If you hire to develop or expand a team or even if you need to replace skills or knowledge gaps for an existing team, hire with these things in mind:

- Choose those with high-quality experience
- Folks who are lifelong learners and self-starters
- Those who also are team players
- Those who are smarter than you
- Those who care about people; who believe in doing the right thing, every time
- Those you would invite home to have dinner with your family

Forget travelogues! Individuals who appear to be successful may not be. The cover looks great, but after a couple of pages you say to yourself what's all this about? If you are recognized among your peers as a professional there is a good chance your reputation is built on true self-confidence and a genuine level of humor and humility. Never believe your own advertising or that about your company. Hype is unhealthy.

Take your backpack. The most important asset in your backpack comes through working in partnership with business leaders. You need to be aware of and appreciate how and why some of the business practices they employ leverage and achieve meaningful benefits for the business.

- Excellent seminars and courses, or a degree, can further solidify your business acumen.
- The facility with which a senior security leader fosters and maintains strong relationships can be indispensable for success.
- Executives are where they are because they are adept at assessing the integrity of relationships. Aligned with the above is team building. Your focus will be on blending diverse security skills in order to make the business—not security—more profitable and a great place to work. You will need both assessment and human resource skills to build and sustain a strong core security team.
- Your project management ability must be strongly coupled with the other items in your backpack.
- You will garner more support, and experience less resistance, if you tailor a project management methodology to fit your company's business initiatives and operations. Managing projects effectively will allow your security team to focus on larger business initiatives, rather than tweaking details.
- Remember: learn how projects are managed in the company.

Trust your compass. Be responsive, be flexible, but stick to your convictions. This is about both commitment and loyalty to the business as well as being able to adjust professionally to deliver meaningful results. Security is in large part a profession of service and the capable security leader sets an example of service for others to follow. Be kind to yourself and to your family. Have faith in those around you; delight in giving them credit whenever you can.

Step back from the fray. Give yourself time to reflect—and not just about business. Take breaks of 3 or 4 days and an annual vacation of at least 2 weeks; you will need it and come back refreshed.

Listen to your gut. Good sound judgment is something that is critical for the security leader. You are in and out of all kinds of sensitive and confidential matters. By knowing yourself well you are more able to effectively share with others how to make the tough calls and at the same time the value you place on their contributions.

Be prepared for long days on the trail—12–14-hour days. This is not made up. This is how it is. If you want to think more about your golf schedule than your businesses schedule, think about another opportunity. Being a security leader today takes a very strong commitment and incredible amounts of energy. Global security leadership at times can push some aspects of the job into the realm of being available 24/7, at least until the right team and processes are in place.

Plan your journey well. Next in importance to building the right team and being in tune with the organization's culture is developing the right strategy. This is crucial to succeed and deliver the best possible security results for the organization. It is the third side of the security success development triangle.

Stay on the trail. Show up every day and work like hell. I learned this from my dad. I added the "like hell" part; his was just "show up every day and work." He was my role model. He outworked everyone else throughout his career. What I learned from him was to be both tenacious and honest. Too many times people with a lot of natural talent do not follow through and complete what they started. Often that is from a lack of confidence or discipline or perhaps both. But you know they will never see the results of what could have been because they do not complete tasks. I hope we all do a better job of finishing what we start. If we honor our commitments, the world will be a better place.

Make your own unique contribution. The very best leaders I have ever been privileged to work with in both government service and private business have always delivered results that contributed to the success of their organization. I have had wider experience in the business world over the last 14 years than I had in my 26 years of government service. The biggest difference between the public and private experiences is if you don't work out in business you are gone; you are history and you are out of there. For the most part business is less loyal and more dollar driven. That's just the way it is—it's not personal, it's just business.

Tell the story. Use a story board to picture for executives exactly how security fits into the budget and operational plan for the corporation. Do not assume that executives automatically understand the contribution security will make to the bottom line. Educate them, and then demonstrate it in action.

Get a bird's eye view. In her book, *Territorial Games*, Annette Simmons suggests that a way to overcome internal turf issues is to bring stakeholders together and invite them to share broad inputs from across the enterprise. Simmons points out that, especially when groups are in transition, initiating changes in a secretive manner "only contributes to peoples' fears." (p. 190)

Draw a tactical map. At whatever point you are in developing a security program for a company, you must be aware of your current location as well as where you've started and where you are going—in other words, keep the destination in view at all times. This applies to the whole enterprise of security leadership as well as to each of its parts. You can only draw a realistic tactical map if you really know the territory, from the office of the chairman to the locations where employees work in the mud. Even more importantly, you can only acquire valid information if people are willing to trust that everything they tell you is business confidential and that the source of the information will not be identified.

Use binoculars. Clarity and collaboration must be based on solid information. To develop a security program you must go after information the same way a business auditor or operational manager does. The information you desire:

- Has to do with inventory balances—not just shrinkage
- With employee and management productivity—not just workplace violence
- With successful hiring practices—not just background checks.

Celebrate roots and wings. Very few corporate security programs are large enough to have a full career progression from point of entry to comprehensive senior leadership opportunities. Excellent employees will move on and celebrate their success while ensuring continuity by looking ahead.

Stand your ground. Sometimes there's no substitute for being assertive. First be patient. However, when the moment comes, I have said: "Look, let's understand something. I don't have any security problems. I'm a very secure guy. But there are security issues in your operations that have a negative effect on the bottom line. If you are not willing to work together on them, that's ok. That's your part of the business, and you are the boss. I don't have time to deal with continual push back. I am here to work with those who want to work with me. I am still willing to do that, but the key words are work together. Think it over. If you change your mind, let me know."

Some are not interested in the trip. Some people will never care about what you do unless they are under physical attack or on their way to jail. In that case, they will notice. If this is the case, let them be. Move on.

Keep your eyes on the horizon. To make progress, you must deliver strategy that produces solid results, but is also flexible and future oriented. I came across just such an approach in the book *Blue Ocean Strategy* by W. Chan Kim and Renee Mauborgne. They state: "Blue oceans denoted all the industries not in existence today." This is the unknown market space. A blue ocean strategy is all about "value innovation"—placing "equal emphasis on value and innovation." They see this as foundational to building an organizationally sound long-term strategy. Blue ocean strategy can be aligned with both known and unknown threats. It is the over-the-horizon security issues that keep some leaders up at night. This book gives you a way to reflect on such challenges. "If you lack an understanding of the opportunity-maximizing and risk-minimizing principles driving the creation and capture of blue oceans, the odds will be lengthened against your blue ocean initiative."

Follow your own road. The organizational dynamics of a given business can often be determined by its infrastructure. Taking the time to learn about various industries is time well spent. Find the environment and culture that are most compatible with your gifts.

Don't be a lone wolf. Be confident enough in your own ability not to try to do everything yourself. To succeed as a security leader in the next generation, seek out those who have successfully made the leap from public to private sector. Make use of every collaborative resource along the way.

Blazing a trail is risky. That is part of the journey. For a further discussion of this aspect of leadership, see *The Very Model of a Modern CSO* by Sherry L. Harowitz, *Security Management* magazine.

And finally, a few closing thoughts. One of the hardest things I have ever undertaken is the writing of this book. I have stuck with it because I have had the benefit of two very different and wonderful careers, in the public and then the private sector. In both arenas, I have been fortunate to have worked with very generous colleagues at all levels, from student interns to government agency heads, from cafeteria workers to chairmen and CEOs.

I have also persevered because in my youth, foundations were laid for doing just that. Someone who has known me since I was a child said: "You know, I have watched you for years and you have taken advantage of every experience since you were a kid. You then blend these experiences into a treasure chest of successes. When faced with very complex issues, you intuitively figure them out; usually you do it by engaging others whose unique gifts complement yours, because they are different than you."

Somehow, someone in your network of friends helps you find the right people, at times through serendipitous circumstances. You successfully recruit others into the project or corporation that needs them. These folks grow. They enjoy their work, and then you or they move on. Best of all, this brings you joy.

It is true that more than anything else I have sought to help others succeed and to rejoice in their success. The teams I have been a part of in both the public and private sectors have shaped this book. Many endeavors today need creative, disciplined, hardworking, and smart public sector leaders to transition into the private sector.

Nowhere is this more important than in the areas of business, community, and NGO security. The opportunity is there. My hope is that as many public sector professionals as possible join us not for just another paycheck, but to make our businesses, communities, and organizations safer and more successful by showing up every day and working like hell!

ABOUT THE AUTHOR

David Quilter's security leadership successes span four decades with contributions in both the public and private sectors. David is both an author and executive consultant as well as a member of the emeritus faculty of the Security Executive Council. His background includes distinguished careers in federal law enforcement and as director of security at several Fortune 500 companies designing asset protection programs and integrating them in ways that enhance profitability. David's cost-recovery tools mitigate business losses, and his leadership in applying smart security principles has transformed security among business leaders and organizations. As an author and presenter David continues to share his wealth of expertise as he works with security leaders around the world.

BIBLIOGRAPHY

Campbell, G. (2011). Measures and metrics in corporate security: A workbook for demonstrating how security adds value to business. Marietta, Georgia (USA). https://www.securityexecutive-council.com/secstore/index.php?main_page=product_info&products_id=324.

Charan, R. (2001). *What the CEO wants you to know: Using your business acumen to understand how your company really works.* New York, NY: Crown Publishing Group.

Dalton, D. R. (2003). *Rethinking corporate security in the post-9/11 era.* Boston, MA: Butterworth–Heinemann.

De Becker, G. (1999). *The gift of fear.* New York, NY: Bantam Books. pp. 84–87.

Drucker, P. F., & Joseph, A. (2006). *Maciariello. The effective executive in action.* New York, NY: HarperCollins.

Harowitz, S. L. (2005). The very model of a modern CSO: Security professionals are forging a new path to ensure that they can be effective stewards of their companies' assets. *Security Management, April,* 42–51.

Kelly, J., & Nadler, S. (2007). Leading from below. *Wall Street Journal, March 3.* (New York, NY)

Kim, W. C., & Mauborgne, R. (2005). *Blue ocean strategy: How to create uncontested market space and make competition irrelevant.* Boston, MA: Harvard Business School Press.

LaFasto, F. M. J., & Larson, C. E. (2001). *When teams work best.* Thousand Oaks, CA: Sage Publications, Inc. (pp. 90–92).

Larson, C. E., & LaFasto, F. M. J. (1989). *Teamwork: What must go right/what can go wrong.* Newberry Park, CA: Sage Publications, Inc.

Simons, R. (2000). *Performance measurement and control systems for implementing strategy.* Upper Saddle River, NJ: Prentice Hall.

Simmons, A. (1997). *Territorial games: Understanding and ending turf wars at work.* New York, NY: Amacom.

Simmons, A. (2007). *Whoever tells the best story wins.* New York, NY: Amacom.

The Wells Report (1996). *Report to the nation on occupational fraud and abuse.* Austin, TX: Association of Certified Fraud Examiners.

Tichy, N. M., & Bennis, W. G. (2007). *Judgment: How winning leaders make great calls.* New York, NY: Portfolio.

Printed and bound by CPI Group (UK) Ltd, Croydon, CR0 4YY

08/05/2025

01864876-0002